Preventing the Clash of Civilizations

Preventing the Clash of Civilizations

A PEACE STRATEGY FOR THE TWENTY-FIRST CENTURY

Roman Herzog

With comments by Amitai Etzioni, Hans Küng, Bassam Tibi, and Masakazu Yamazaki

Edited by Henrik Schmiegelow

St. Martin's Press
New York

PREVENTING THE CLASH OF CIVILIZATIONS

 For information, address St. Martin's Press, 175 Fifth Avenue, New York, N.Y. 10010.

ISBN 0-312-22444-3

Library of Congress Cataloging-in-Publication Data
Herzog, Roman, 1934-
Preventing the clash of civilizations : a peace strategy for the twenty-first century / Roman Herzog with comments by Amitai Etzioni . . . [et al.] ; edited by Henrik Schmiegelow.
p. cm.
Includes bibliographical references and index.
ISBN 0-312-22444-3 (cloth)
1. International relations and culture. 2. Peace. I. Etzioni, Amitai. II. Schmiegelow, Henrik. III. Title.
JZ1251.H47 1999
327.1'7—dc21 99-21773
CIP

Design by Acme Art, Inc.

First edition: May, 1999
10 9 8 7 6 5 4 3 2 1

Contents

PART II
COMMENTS

Preface

This book presents statements by the President of the Federal Republic of Germany, Roman Herzog, on inter-cultural relations. It also includes comments by four scholars, Amitai Etzioni, Hans Küng, Bassam Tibi, and Masakazu Yamazaki. Their common concern is to prevent the "clash of civilizations" scenario from becoming reality. Since this scenario is an intellectual projection that has had considerable influence on the perceptions of policy-making elites, the obvious strategy for preventing its realization is to mobilize ideas of peaceful cooperation as a countervailing force against mindsets of conflict and violence.

Naturally, a head of state's focus and style differ from those of a scholar. The head of state will take a more normative and strategic approach, looking at how reality *ought* to evolve in the future, whereas the scholar will make his point by analyzing the object of his research as it *is*. In the case of this book, however, the head of state is also a scholar (of law) by profession and inclination, and the commenting scholars are not only known for their analytical insights but also for their normative commitments. Not surprisingly, our goal is to combine statements of theory and statements of policy.

It is important to know that the German head of state has no executive power and thus must take care not to interfere with his government's prerogatives in foreign as well as domestic policy. But in the fifty years of the existence of the Federal Republic of Germany its successive heads of state have developed a pattern of using their own constitutional right of free speech to draw the public's attention to long-term problems of the polity, the economy, the society, and culture not in the immediate focus of day-to-day government policies, domestic or foreign. In that way some of post-war Germany's presidents have exerted a considerable measure of what is known in political science as "soft power."

President Herzog has taken a keen interest in the renaissance of cultures following the collapse of the bipolar system. At the same time he has used numerous occasions to rally support for a strategy of preventing inter-cultural conflict by focussing on the commonalities between cultures. In his opening address to the World Economic Forum in Davos in January 1995 he explained the basic concept for this "diplomacy of inter-cultural understanding" for the first time:

> It has often been said that common institutions are impossible without a common civilization and that no such civilization exists. I would like to conclude with the thesis that a common civilization does indeed exist—at least to a considerable extent. The frequently invoked "clashes of civilizations" are not "clashes" between Buddhist, Christian, Confucian, Hindu, Islamic, and other religions, but between fundamentalism and enlightenment, dogmatism and pragmatism, civilized behavior and uncivilized behavior within each of these cultures. Only if the civilized majorities of all countries and cultures were to let their fundamentalist minorities have their way for too long could the scenario of a global cultural conflict become reality.
>
> The universal civilization is identifiable by an ethical core common to all cultures. It is already embodied in a highly developed form in the Charter of the United Nations and in the 1948 Universal Declaration of Human Rights. Kant's categorical imperative includes it as well. But there is also a proverb that is familiar to nearly all human beings in the world.

> It is the Golden Rule, which can be found in the teachings of Confucius, in the seven basic ethical rules observed by Buddhists, in the Mahabharata, the Indian national epic, as well as in the Bible: "Do not do unto others what you would not like them to do unto you." When the United Nations was founded after the end of the Second World War, everyone knew what this rule meant. The risks confronting us today are hardly of lesser magnitude. Let us therefore comply with the Golden Rule, which conforms to both our own interest and to morality. We have yet to find a better one.

With this concept as his guide, President Herzog has pursued his intellectual diplomacy during state visits to countries that identify themselves with one or several of the major cultures of the world, with speeches on inter-cultural issues at home and abroad, with the publication of articles and books, and finally, with the initiative of a joint patronage of eight Western and Islamic leaders for a network of academic institutions engaging in research on ways to promote understanding between Islamic and Western cultures.

In the first seven chapters of this book some of the steps of this diplomacy are presented as answers to salient questions of inter-cultural relations rather than in chronological order. A short chronological survey of these steps may thus be useful.

In an address to students of the university of Islamabad during his state visit to Pakistan in April 1995, President Herzog paid tribute to the important contributions of the poet and philosopher Mohamed Iqbal and of the founder of modern Pakistan, Jinnah, to the spread of the ideas of tolerance and democracy (chapter 1).

In July 1995, while receiving President Jiang Zemin of the People's Republic of China, he recalled that Confucius and Socrates lived in the same century, and though they knew nothing of each other's existence, they both concerned themselves with the same humanity, the same reason, the same pursuit of knowledge, the same distinction between good and evil, and the same need to vanquish injustice and violence. He congratulated the Chinese Foreign Minister for having assured China's South-East Asian neighbors at a conference in May 1995 that China's foreign policy would be guided by the same golden rule he himself had invoked four months earlier in Davos (chapter 4).

In October 1995 President Herzog was asked to offer a tribute on the occasion of the award of the 1995 peace prize of the German book trade association to Annemarie Schimmel, one of the major Western scholars of Islamic literature and philosophy. He used this opportunity to warn the intellectual elite of Germany and other Western countries not to be misguided by hostile Western depictions of Islam, and called for inter-cultural dialogue as an alternative to global culture wars (chapter 2).

In September 1996 President Herzog published an article on the transcultural validity of human rights in the German weekly *Die Zeit.* In this article he proposed to differentiate between the core of human rights (such as the protection against torture, serfdom, discrimination according to race, faith etc.) that need to be recognized universally and a wider set of social and economic rights that are evidently subject to cultural variation. This article paved the way for an open discussion of the subject of human rights with the Chinese leadership during President Herzog's state visit to China in November 1996 (chapter 3).

In April 1997 President Herzog paid state visits to Malaysia and Japan. In Kuala Lumpur he took part in a colloquium at the Institute of Islamic Understanding that discussed the possibility of the emergence of a universal civilization that would be the result of contributions of all cultures (chapter 5). Addressing faculty and students of the Waseda University in Tokyo, he invoked the pragmatic harmony of Confucianism, Buddhism, Shintoism, and even Christianity in the lives of Japanese individuals and households to refute the alleged inevitability of conflict between cultures. He also reflected on the similarity of some of the strains in Japanese and German society as a consequence of demographic developments and proposed the application of the Golden Rule to the relation between old and young generations in both countries (chapter 4).

In September 1998, a state visit to South Korea offered President Herzog the opportunity to honor President Kim Dae Jung both for his long struggle for democracy in Korea and for his compelling argument that democracy is not merely a Western culture but has its autonomous roots in Asian cultures as well. He explained how market economics and democracy could mutually strengthen each other in a culturally pluralistic world (chapter 6).

Finally, when he opened the World Economic Forum in Davos for the second time, in January 1999, he offered the vision of a world in which transnational, national, and multilateral policy-makers would consider it to be in their own best interest to abide by an imperative of responsibility for an emerging global political system. He emphasized the importance of inter-cultural dialogue to attain this goal. More particularly, he applauded the Iranian President Mohammad Khatami for having called on Islamic societies not to hide inside the fortress of tradition but to open up to the modern world without falling prey to unbridled materialism. He invited worldwide support for President Khatami's call for a dialogue between the religions and his initiative for an "international year of dialogue" (chapter 7).

The second part of the book is intended to invite debate on the issues addressed by President Herzog. The four scholars who agreed to contribute their comments come from very different cultural backgrounds and academic disciplines. There are, of course, significant points on which they disagree with each other or with President Herzog. It is all the more remarkable, however, that they do agree on the need to refocus the debate in order to prevent the scenario of the clash of civilizations from becoming a self-fulfilling prophecy.

Amitai Etzioni, the American political scientist and leading voice of communitarianism, explores the depth of the tension between cultural diversity and universal moral values. He shows that the necessary recognition of cultural pluralism does not justify moral relativism. On the other hand he emphasizes that no culture has a monopoly of moral claims on other cultures. Like President Herzog, Professor Etzioni believes that there is a connection between economic and political development and that, more particularly, open societies around the world are flourishing to a far greater extent than closed societies (chapter 8).

Hans Küng, German theologist and indefatigable builder of ethical bridges among Christian denominations as well as among all great religions of the world, begins by doing justice to Samuel Huntington, the author of the scenario of "the clash of civilizations." He recognizes that the scenario had at least the merit of drawing attention to the importance of religion in world politics. On the other hand he criticizes the scenario as a model of power and conflict in the tradition of political realism with too little attention to the alternative worldview, namely a world of cooperation and peace. He proposes a compromise between the two views and notes with gratification that Professor Huntington himself has moved in the direction of such a compromise in his 1997 book that elaborates his scenario (chapter 9). Indeed, Huntington recognized the importance of focusing on the same commonalities among cultures that President Herzog had emphasized in January 1995 in Davos.

Bassam Tibi, a Muslim born in Damascus who became a German Professor of international relations, is himself something of a living example of inter-cultural understanding. He, too, feels that Professor Huntington's scenario should be taken seriously. He emphasizes that it is necessary to recognize cultural differences as they are. But like President Herzog he warns against the danger that fundamentalists politicize religious differences and thus move the clash of civilizations from the potential to the actual.

Unlike Hans Küng, he does not believe in a "world ethos." His preferred method of maintaining peace among cultures is to promote understanding and respect of cultural diversity through inter-cultural dialogue. Yet Bassam Tibi, too, stresses at least one important inter-cultural commonality. He introduces his contribution by highlighting the distinction between reason and faith that is common to Western and Islamic philosophy (chapter 10).

Masakazu Yamazaki, the sociologist who drew the world's attention to the fact that there is such a thing as Japanese individualism, concludes the book with a view from East Asia. His contribution stands out by questioning the importance of religions as a source of international conflict. Like President Herzog in his speech at Waseda University (chapter 4), he simply points to the peaceful coexistence of Confucianism, Buddhism, Islam, and Christianity in many East-Asian nations. The real conflict, he argues, arises between rich and poor within cultures, be they Western or otherwise. He explains that there are two moral systems in the world, a "commercial ethics" and a "political ethics." He believes that each nation-state needs to find its own balance between these two moral systems (chapter 11).

Originally it was planned to offer a final comment from Samuel Huntington, who rightly felt that having triggered the whole debate by his *Foreign Affairs* article of 1993, he could claim the right of the last word. Unfortunately he was unable to send us his contribution in time for this book. But he asked us to convey his full support to President Herzog for his strategy of preventing the clash of civilizations by focusing on commonalities among cultures.

PART I

Statements by President Roman Herzog

CHAPTER 1

Commonalities between Islamic and Western Cultures

(Speech before the Department of International Relations of the Quaid-e-Azam University of Islamabad, 5 April 1995)

[. . .] MY STATE VISIT TO PAKISTAN takes me to a country with a sophisticated cultural tradition. As long as five thousand years ago, early civilizations developed here which were equal to the high cultures of the Nile and Euphrates. Later your country formed the bridge across which the spirit of Ancient Greece was to enter the subcontinent, a spirit which for a time played a major role in molding local cultures, for example that of the Ghandara. The great Mogul dynasty left contemporary Pakistan wondrous buildings and other monuments to Man's ingenuity [. . .]

Almost no one has thought as deeply about relations between our two cultures as your great poet and thinker, Mohammed Iqbal, a hundred years ago. We are proud that Iqbal spent some of his student years in Germany, and that German culture furnished this great scholar with some important ideas, which have also been of benefit to us, since Iqbal, in his notes, left us much that is worthy of consideration with regard to Germany and its classical literature and philosophy. His dictum with reference to Goethe, "Our soul discovers itself when we come into contact with a great mind," can also be applied to the philosopher himself: Through the eyes of this scholar our view of your country is also enhanced. [. . .]

But I am not only here to make a journey into a distant historical past, attractive as this prospect may be. Our two countries are fellow players, co-shapers and equal partners in the major political developments which characterize our age.

In Germany, over the last weeks, we have been commemorating the fiftieth anniversary of the end of the Second World War. Seven weeks ago I held a speech in Dresden, a place which like no other challenges us to consider the atrocities of any war. At that time I said, "We remember those who were persecuted and killed because they belonged to another nation or another race. . . . We remember those who lost their lives because they resisted tyranny and those who died because they remained true to their convictions or their faith."

You, too, commemorated yesterday, a date which stands for an important and tragic event in Pakistan's recent history. You, too, recalled what important and indeed indispensable assets freedom of thought and freedom from political persecution are.

Sharing these values is a central element of our friendship and of Pakistan-German relations. Our two governments observe the rule of law over injustice as well as the freedom of those who hold differing views. They respect our responsibility toward the great tasks of our time, such as the fight against famine and poverty, the protection of the environment and the natural resources of our planet, as well as the preservation or, where necessary, restoration of peace.

I come from a country which has been especially deeply affected by the epochal changes of the late 1980s and which is still in a state of transformation. I am aware of the great sympathy with which the Pakistan people followed the process of German reunification, and I would like to express my sincere gratitude to them for this support.

I do not intend to expound at length on German foreign policy, but I would like to say that the new, united Germany remains committed to the same values as Germany prior to the fall of the Berlin Wall: The widening and deepening of the European Union, the further development of the Atlantic Alliance, support for the United Nations, and all tendencies toward regional integration, the promotion of sustainable development in the countries of the southern hemisphere, to name but a few.

By comparison with the old Federal Republic, the new Germany has become larger in both territorial and economic terms, and thus also politically more important. We have grown, beyond any doubt, and we are prepared to assume our increased international responsibilities. But we are perfectly capable of being realistic about our options and abilities. Terms such as "great power" or "Europe's leading power" have been coined by others, not by us. Modesty becomes us well, and I am prepared to say this to my countrymen when necessary.

One of the main thrusts of German foreign policy was, and is, cooperation with the countries of Africa, Latin America, and Asia, with Asia naturally playing a special role.

The Federal Republic of Germany has, especially in recent times, made considerable efforts to appraise Asia's significance for its foreign policy. In October 1993 the Federal Government adopted the Concept on Asia which takes account of the latest developments in the Asia-Pacific region. This Concept is the necessary answer to the obvious shifting of the political and economic balance toward Asia, by far the most dynamic growth region of our age. We Europeans want to adjust to this fact. After years of concentrating on East-West relations and the reunification process, we Germans in particular would do well to pay greater attention to the truly breathtaking developments occurring in this part of the world and to draw the appropriate conclusions for policy.

At the beginning of 1994 the German ambassadors to the Asia-Pacific region met in Bonn at a conference, chaired by the Federal Minister for Foreign Affairs, during which the new Concept on Asia was discussed. Guidelines for implementing the Concept were also drawn up. My predecessor, former Federal President von Weizsäcker, gave a reception for the ambassadors and listened to their first-hand reports on your continent's development and future opportunities. An essential element of our new policy on Asia from the start was an increase in the exchange of high-level and top-level visits. My visit to Pakistan, which is also my first state-visit, by the way, forms part of this concept. It takes me to one of our most important Asian partners and is thus another sign of our renewed awareness of the significance of Asia.

We want to learn much more about this continent and about your country and to concern ourselves even more closely with it. We hope that we can succeed in better adjusting to Asia and thus also to our partner country Pakistan. It should be the common objective of both the EU and the Asian countries to continually exchange views on the burning issues and problems of our age. For example our shared responsibilities for securing peace; for cooperating to combat international crime, drug-trafficking, and the proliferation of weapons of mass destruction; and for resolving conflicts by negotiation. Europe does not seek a say in Asia, and comparatively small Germany certainly does not. However, in a world that is becoming smaller, with its constantly increasing global links, conflicts in seemingly remote corners of the world have an effect on other countries. This is why we are concerned when conflicts on a continent or subcontinent endanger regional stability, whether in Africa, Latin America, Asia, or in our own backyard, in Europe.

Our political cooperation with Asia has long since become a vital part of our global policy of securing peace. Due to their global political weight, the Asian states are becoming more and more important in settling conflicts. This applies not least to United Nations tasks. Let me take this opportunity to express my recognition of Pakistan's exemplary contribution to UN peace-keeping measures.

German business, too, has long since adapted to the new situation. The Asia Pacific Committee of German Business, in which numerous leading German business figures are involoved, shows the extent of the attention this growth region is attracting.

The Asia-Pacific region, of which Pakistan forms an important part, is entering the twenty-first century with a huge potential for the future. Almost 60 percent of the world's population live in Asia. Large markets are already in existence, and truly gigantic ones are in the making. With annual growth of 7 to 8 percent expected for the foreseeable future, Asia, as I have already mentioned, is the world's most dynamic region. Over a quarter of global GNP is already being produced in this area of the world; in ten years this could rise to a third. Today Asian trade already accounts for a quarter of all world trade. The transpacific exchange of goods has for years exceeded transatlantic trade, and it is still rising.

In the technology field Asian companies have secured for themselves leading international positions. Asian banks and stock exchanges play an increasing role in the global financial markets. Over a third of the world's currency reserves are deposited in Asian central banks.

We Europeans should learn a lesson from all this. Asia's rise should be seen as an opportunity and a benefit, and not just as a challenge. To make plans that ignore Asia is to ignore the future. What especially interests me, and what I hope to learn from you during my visit, is the question of what role Pakistan has come to play within this growth region.

At first sight the growth rates of the countries in the subcontinent are lower than those of the "economic motors" in the ASEAN countries or of some large East Asian economies. However, the countries of the subcontinent in particular have the chance to further develop their potential in terms of human and natural resources in close and peaceful cooperation. In the South Asian Association for Regional Cooperation Pakistan has, together with its neighbors, created the appropriate framework for this development. With 1.3 billion people, that is a quarter of the total world population, SAARC is one of the world's largest regional organizations. Your country can rightly be proud that one of the first major SAARC institutions, the Chamber of Commerce and Industry, will be based in Karachi.

Germany has given the foundation and development of this regional organization strong political support and has initiated dialogue between the European Union and SAARC, as it has also done in the case of ASEAN and other regional bodies. I am pleased that in 1993 a first meeting took place between the EU Commission and a SAARC delegation. Indeed, last year in New York, Federal Foreign Minister Kinkel, in his former capacity as President of the European Council, formally opened the political dialogue with the Chairman of the SAARC Council and offered to intensify and deepen political cooperation in a spirit of partnership. I would be happy if this offer were taken up and pursued. Perhaps the forthcoming SAARC summit in New Delhi will provide an opportunity to take a position on this issue.

I presume that the possibilities and opportunities this regional organization provides for the subcontinent are by no means exhausted. I am not merely referring to economics, but also in particular to the political sphere. As a friend of Pakistan and of the region as a whole, I would like to encourage you to make enhanced use of the institutional framework provided by SAARC for the objectives of regional stabilization and conflict management. Europe's recent history shows how some countries which were "arch-enemies" only half a century before have come to enjoy mutual confidence, functioning cooperation, and even friendship through common economic and trade policies.

In the case of the subcontinent, this may seem an unlikely perspective to you at this moment. However, I am sure that after many years of the atrocities of war and hatred in Europe, the founding fathers of the European Community could not imagine how cooperation between the member states would look in practice. But they had a vision, and with hindsight we can say it was a blessing for Europe. Therefore the SAARC states, too, should explore all possible avenues in order to achieve forms of political cooperation enabling SAARC to settle existing disputes between members in a peaceful manner.

Probably the most important conflict, one which has burdened and paralyzed the political, but also economic and societal, development of the entire subcontinent for almost half a century now, is the Kashmir issue. This will of course also feature strongly in my talks here. Germany, and this also applies to the European Union as a whole, has traditionally maintained friendly relations with both Pakistan and India. The Federal Government makes a point of using the same language and arguments in its dialogue with both the Pakistan and Indian governments. We are taking pains not to favor either side over the other in this friendly network of relations.

The European Union is following the Kashmir issue with great concern. It has repeatedly recommended to both sides that they settle their conflict by means of bilateral negotiations, or at least take initial pragmatic steps to limit the scope of the dispute. I would like to earnestly reiterate this recommendation here today. It would be a significant first step if both governments could bring themselves to resume their dialogue as soon as possible.

Germany is not blind to the daily human rights violations in Kashmir. The European Union has time and again reminded the conflict parties of their duty to uphold human rights. This reminder is directed at all those involved. I expressly welcome the assurance given by the Pakistan government that it does not render logistic and materiel assistance in this conflict.

I am firmly convinced that the Kashmir issue cannot be settled militarily, but only politically with the agreement of all parties involved. An imposed settlement would not stand the test of time, but would only lead to renewed tension.

As a nation divided for decades, we Germans attach special significance to the right to self-determination. We ourselves have always demanded this right, using peaceful means alone, in the course of our post-war history. Our experience shows that the right to self-determination should not be enforced by violent means, if it is to endure, but that it must be realized as part of a lasting order of peace. This order is not, however, to be had without effort. It may arise as a result of a change in the general political situation. But it must above all be earned the hard way: by creating trust, guarding against all negative eventualities, showing willingness to compromise and a great deal of goodwill. This, too, can be gleaned from my country's recent history.

In two weeks' time the Non-Proliferation Treaty Review and Extension Conference will open in New York. Germany and the European Union attach great significance to this meeting. The Federal Government and its partners call for the indefinite and unconditional extension of the NPT. We see in its strict observance the decisive instrument for preventing a nuclear arms race and for protecting the human race from destroying itself by nuclear means.

It is therefore only logical that we appeal to all nations of the world to accede to the NPT. The fact that the two most important states of the subcontinent have up to now kept their distance from the Treaty and, as nonmembers, will not take part in the New York conference does not make us very hopeful. I am aware of the reasons and concerns which in Pakistan's view prevent it from acceding to the Non-Proliferation Treaty. But I would like to encourage you--and we are saying the same to the Indian government--to be aware of your great responsibility for the stability, not only of the region, but of the whole world, and to accede to the NPT.

One of the values we share is the freedom to choose one's religion, a right which should be exercised without fear of punishment. The great founder of Pakistan, Jinnah, has a legendary reputation in Germany because, among other things, he steadfastly advocated religious tolerance. The very founding of Pakistan itself, if I am not mistaken, was a result of the desire for political and religious self-determination. For this reason I am particularly pleased that your government, as the foreign minister of Pakistan confirmed in mid-February in Geneva, intends to accede to major international human rights and civil rights agreements and to put an end to the abuse of the so-called blasphemy clause by adopting appropriate legislation.

We Germans, too, are obliged to uphold human rights, and we, too, are subject to the scrutiny of other countries. You know as well as I do that we in Germany have had to deal with serious problems, by which I mean the outbreaks of xenophobia which have occurred there (these have, however, been the work of a small group of incorrigibles). These perpetrators of violence are being brought to court and face the full force of our penal code. Although the attacks on foreigners also met with protest from abroad, it was the Germans themselves who immediately expressed their continuing disgust at and wholehearted rejection of these acts. The peaceful coexistence of nations can only be credibly preached abroad when it is practiced at home. Let me take this opportunity to reaffirm that we want Germany to remain a place where people are happy to live and where they can do so free from harassment and antipathy. Germany is and will remain a cosmopolitan country.

I do not share Samuel Huntington's view that the clash of civilizations is inevitable and determines our planet's political future. Nothing would be more dangerous for the nations of West and East than to prepare for a supposed confrontation between Islam and Christianity. I regard it as damaging and completely inappropriate even to spread such ideas. The great thinkers both here and in the West have constantly pointed to the links between the Orient and the Occident. I need only recall what Mohammed Iqbal said about the interrelation between Western values and Islam: "The most remarkable phenomenon of modern history is the enormous speed at which the world of Islam is approaching the West on intellectual issues. There is nothing wrong with this, since in intellectual terms European culture is merely a further development of some of the most important phases of Islamic culture." Let us not forget that the founder of modern Pakistan, Jinnah, emphasized that there is no conflict between Islam and democracy. Fifty years ago he described the principles of Islamic democracy as being the equality of all human beings, justice and fair play towards all. Since then these values have lost none of their relevance. Thus to fabricate antagonisms between Islam and democracy is an arbitrary act, often done for ulterior motives and, in many cases, even with evil in mind. Our aim should not be the clash of cultures or civilizations but the development of a common civilization built on consensus and mutual trust.

The necessity imposed upon us all, that of together mastering the great future challenges facing mankind, leaves us no room for drifting apart. Global problems demand global solutions and thus also close, trusting cooperation between all inhabitants of this planet.

CHAPTER 2

Inter-Cultural Dialogue versus Global Culture Wars

(Speech on the Occasion of the Award of the 1995 Peace Prize of the German Book Trade Association to Annemarie Schimmel, Frankfurt, 15 October 1995)

THERE IS NO NEED TO STRESS that this year's award of the Peace Prize of the German Book Trade Association has been accompanied by fierce controversy; it is plain for all to see.

However, the course which the discussion in this context has taken gives me reason to hope. After an unfortunate beginning, which was certainly not to anyone's credit, a debate has developed which has helped to deepen understanding in more than one respect. I believe I am right in saying that it has overcome the usual divides. It has reminded both the supporters and the opponents of today's prize-winner that political correctness cannot be a legitimate barrier to the constitutionally guaranteed freedom of speech. It has prompted scholars to leave their studies to make public statements. It has already led us to recognize that it is vital on foreign-policy and domestic grounds that we engage in an intensive and discriminating study of Islam. And it has, after all, already added to our knowledge; who among us could really have said before the controversy about Annemarie Schimmel what sufism is or—even more importantly—by what criteria a fatwa should be judged?

The Peace Prize of the German Book Trade Association follows in the tradition of the Enlightenment, and it serves, as its name suggests, to promote peace—peace between human beings, between peoples, and certainly also between the great cultural and intellectual traditions in this world but which have recently gained a new profile and self-confidence of astonishing, even dramatic, proportions.

In our own vicinity we sense the immediacy of the challenge posed by Islam. And Judaism has accompanied us for an entire millennium, in good and in bad times. However, there are other religions and cultures which influence hundreds of millions of hearts and minds and which also have a strong new self-awareness: Buddhism, Hinduism, and Confucianism, to mention only the major ones.

It may be that our common ground resulting from science, technology, and global information, from worldwide economic interdependence and perhaps even from newly emerging security structures prevent the rash predictions of an impending "clash of civilizations" from coming true. However, living together in harmony and in humane conditions requires more than that.

It demands first and foremost a fervent endeavour to ensure that the boundaries between cultures do not remain, or develop into, permanent divides between rich and poor; for this reason I advocate wherever possible free markets, economic cooperation, and, in the interests of the poorest nations, development aid. Secondly, it demands tireless efforts to bring to light and strengthen existing but hidden similarities and to foster, and where necessary fight for, ideas which, as experience has shown, are conducive to peace.

I am sure you know what I mean by this: I am talking of the struggle for, as well as the tireless and undaunted promotion of, human rights to which the international community has, after all, committed itself. Let us not forget that these rights evolved relatively slowly and laboriously in the West, too, and suffered repeated terrible setbacks. There is still a considerable gap between aspirations and reality in Western cultures also—I need only remind you of women's rights. Nevertheless, we know today that human rights are the most convincing concept capable of creating peace between individuals, peoples, and states, and thus ultimately also between cultures.

To this end, peoples and cultures must learn more about each other. Without this mutual knowledge there can be no mutual understanding; without mutual understanding there can be no mutual respect and no trust; and without trust there can be no peace but, indeed, really only the risk of a clash.

Countless very different efforts are therefore needed if peace is to be accomplished and, above all, preserved. And every earnest endeavour is worthy of praise. Some have said that although they hold Frau Schimmel in high regard as a scholar, they cannot understand why her academic work on literature, on ancient texts, deserves a Peace Prize. I say to them: In the darkest period of German history it was not least British, American, and Russian literary scholars and scholars of German who in their own way conveyed a different, and today we would say a more valid, understanding of German culture than the official Germany of that era. It is not least this selfless and at that time certainly "unpolitical" work which made a distinct contribution towards subsequent peace and reconciliation. No one who interpreted verses from "Don Carlos" or "Egmont" in Oxford or Harvard in those days was lending respectability to German totalitarianism by doing so. Precisely the fact that we are here today to mark the award of the Peace Prize of the German Book Trade Association should also make us appreciate what the study of literature and intellectual life can do to promote peace and reconciliation.

This is borne out very clearly in our current relationship with Islam. It would hardly be doing the German public an injustice to claim that too many of us mainly associate terms such as "inhumane penal law," "religious intolerance," "suppression of women," and "aggressive fundamentalism" with the word "Islam." However, we must revise this narrow view. Let us recall for a moment that six or seven hundred years ago there was a great Islamic enlightenment which brought a considerable amount of classical knowledge to the West and which, in turn, found itself confronted with Western thinking, which it must have regarded as quite fundamentalist and intolerant.

There is more: For example, the sufic currents in Islamic thinking on which Annemarie Schimmel places special emphasis and which add much greater depth and subtlety to it than the familiar distinction between Sunna and Shiah. And we should finally realize that the Islamic world, just like our own, is not a monolithic bloc and least of all a fundamentalist bloc. Thus, for example, Indonesian Islam is something quite different from Iranian Islam, and Indonesia is, after all, the largest Islamic country today. Have we, to mention another example, taken note of the fact that the Presidents of the six Turkic-speaking countries, who met recently to formulate publicly the common principles of their policy, included secularism among them? Do we realize that, as Annemarie Schimmel has shown us time and again, many things which we, in common with most Muslims, attribute to Islam are not laid down in the Koran?

Views will always have to differ on what this means for our attitude towards Islam. However, no one can deny that it gives us a clearer and, above all, fairer picture, which makes it easier to engage in cross-cultural talks. And I would like to reiterate that this will not only make us more aware of the importance of Islam in the world, but also profoundly influence our relationship with the Muslims living in our country.

Probably the term "fundamentalism," which comes so easily to our lips, is in itself so ambiguous that it is misleading.

Those who speak of "fundamentalism" today usually, and not always without reason, associate it with the humiliation of women, inhumane punishment for thieves and adulteresses, and attacks on writers and journalists who have fallen into disfavor. In reality, what we commonly describe as fundamentalism is nothing but an instrumentalization of religious sentiments for political purposes, a blatant bid for totalitarian power. The threat of this abuse of religion is particularly prevalent where social hardship and a lack of established rights offer a breeding ground for manipulation of the masses.

Let me repeat in this context what I have said earlier: These are phenomena which we cannot accept under any circumstances nor tolerate for foreign-policy reasons or on the grounds of a weakly ethical relativism. When we enter into a dialogue with others we bring in some basic precepts which are not negotiable. These include freedom of speech, which means above all that no one should suffer harm as a result of his convictions. A long, often bloody and cruel history has taught us Europeans that these rights must never again be put at stake. This is why we cannot accept death threats towards someone for writing a book. I would like to say to those who believe that this represents a minority Western view wrongly claiming universal validity: Dialogue can only take place where no one has to fear imprisonment, torture, or murder for any comment he has made. This rule is neither Western nor Eastern nor in any other way related to geography. It is *the* fundamental conceptual prerequisite for dialogue.

And in order to ensure that no one thinks I only mean this in abstract and general terms, let me say quite specifically: Whoever threatens to kill Salman Rushdie or anyone else because of a literary text should see in us an adamant opponent. We shall stand by anyone threatened with death or torture. I therefore take this opportunity to urge the men responsible for the murder threats against writers such as Salman Rushdie to honestly and reliably withdraw these threats and, in particular, the wretched promise of a bounty.

But it must also be said in all clarity that remarks among ourselves pointing out the distress of many devout Muslims concerning something which they regard as blasphemous cannot be prohibited.

This is precisely the reason why I believe that when we talk about fundamentalism among ourselves we are far from agreed on what we mean by it. Matters are relatively straightforward when only considering these violations: We know from our own experience that they are common human rights violations that must therefore quite simply and without any further discussion be denounced and treated as serious crimes. The "only" question here is what consequences we are to draw from this in our foreign policy. Protest, political sanctions, or patient but unequivocal canvassing for our positions? I believe that each of these paths is legitimate. However, we must always examine which of them will be most effective in a concrete situation.

Yet, this may touch even deeper sentiments. I have already spoken of the Islamic enlightenment, which probably clashed with opposite standpoints in our Christian world, standpoints we ourselves would today describe as Christian fundamentalism. Could it be that our positions today are reversed? Do we find it so difficult to come to terms with Islam because it is often based on a profound popular devoutness while we ourselves live in a largely secularized world? And how, if I am right, do we live with this dissent? Do we in all seriousness want to identify devout

Muslims with violent fundamentalists merely because we ourselves no longer know or at least no longer seem to know how it feels to have one's religious sentiments mocked?

I am not at all in favor of ethical relativism on our part in this context. Plurality and tolerance are certainly important values which I would not want to relinquish under any circumstances. However, if they are to work they must be realistic and honest. This means that one must know and understand the positions held by others and, at the same time, have a standpoint of one's own in order to be able to tolerate that of others. Ethical relativism alone leads to a complete loss of standards, rather than to tolerance.

I repeat that for us human rights are indispensable: The dignity of the individual, the inviolability of human life, prohibition of torture and corporal punishment, personal freedom, equality of men and women before the law, freedom of thought, religion and ideological convictions; I do not intend to complete the list here. These convictions, which we gained and consolidated as a result of our terrible experiences in the past, cannot be subject to any modification.

However, every international debate on human rights also shows that professing convictions and voicing protest alone does not suffice in the discourse among cultures.

Long experience tells me that our endeavours to make our position understood must extend far beyond merely professing convictions and voicing protest. And here again knowledge of and understanding for our partners is what counts.

All cultures and religions we encounter in the world have common or at least related ideas and principles—although their sources may differ considerably. It is not particularly ingenious to always, and immediately, refer in this context to the Golden Rule which can be described by the proverb "Do not do unto others what you would not like them to do unto you"—a precept common to all cultures. However, if we could only to some extent succeed in making this Golden Rule the maxim of practical politics, that in itself would be an excellent point of departure for safeguarding international peace and no less the rights of the individual! And that is not the only starting point which comes to mind. A symposium of academics and philosophers from all over the world and from many different cultures which took place a few weeks ago in Bellevue Castle, my official Berlin residence, led me to consider many more intellectual resources. These resources, in conjunction with common economic interests in open markets, the knowledge imparted equally by the natural sciences all over the world, and the new possibilities offered worldwide by the information age could be developed into something which could spare us a global clash of cultures. It is worthwhile, in my view, to seek the greatest inter-cultural common denominator.

The quest for a cross-cultural ethical minimum does not mean that we should content ourselves with this minimum in our own sphere. Naturally, the same applies to other cultures. Nor does this quest require us to refrain from continuing to fight for and promote our own concepts of human dignity and human rights. However, we, just as all others, could do so in peace, and, most importantly, no one would have to fear this anymore as an extension of traditional colonial rule by ideological means.

It may be that I am dreaming a dream which will not be fulfilled, at least not during our lifetime. However, the terrible vision of a global culture conflict makes it impossible for us not to undertake any attempt at all.

The question arises as to whether or not all states and cultures have a common interest in ensuring that this scenario does not become a self-fulfilling prophesy. Can the inter-cultural dialogue now become part of a rational strategy for peace?

There are indications that the supposed "clash of civilizations" is actually a "clash of political fundamentalisms" in which the moderate majorities of the populations concerned are by no means interested. The question is whether today cross-cultural cooperation among defenders of enlightenment, pragmatists, and those seeking a civilization based on reconciliation could serve as a rational strategy for peace against those who evoke enemy images. And this dialogue calls for the kind of people who move among and impart knowledge about cultures, who are willing and able to understand different concepts and experiences and to convey what they have learned to others, to build bridges of trust.

Annemarie Schimmel is such a person. That is why she deserves the Peace Prize. She loves the Islamic intellectual world and this love is returned by many Muslims for that very reason; it is wrong and unjust to regard this as sympathy for political fundamentalism. She herself describes, in her book "Mystische Dimension des Islams," the dispute among Islamic mystics, the aforementioned sufis, and orthodox Muslims who always felt uneasy about the sufis. Their mystical imagination and "inner Islam," as it was described by the orientalist Titus Burckhardt, do not lend themselves to fundamentalist or orthodox thinking. On the contrary, the Islamic mystics were, as Frau Schimmel has convincingly shown, persecuted time and again because they regarded themselves as the genuine upholders of freedom in a hostile environment of religious legalism.

Although it is quite tempting, I do not want to speculate about possible parallels between sufism and Christian pietism, especially as regards their striving for social improvement. For me as a layman the evidence is convincing: It was not until I read Frau Schimmel's books that I began to learn something of the breathtaking diversity of movements within Islam in the past and present. And perhaps some of you have felt the same. That would mean that we all have a lot to catch up on in our knowledge and understanding of others. We cannot afford to ignore the breathtaking diversity of movements within Islam; that would ultimately only strengthen those who aim to stifle differentiated thinking. Therefore let us not make the work of political fundamentalists easier by conjuring up a uniform Islam which does not exist. On world politico-cultural grounds, if you will forgive this monstrous expression, we have no choice but to learn more about the Islamic world if we seriously intend to protect human rights and democracy.

If, as Frau Schimmel has shown us, we try to understand another culture this does not mean that we become immersed in it. We can only reach an understanding from our own standpoint. If we give up our own standpoint in order to foster understanding then there will be nothing left to understand and no more differences to be discussed. We can only be genuinely curious about Islam and its rich culture if and because our own culture is different.

Frau Schimmel aroused this curiosity in me and I hope that many others have experienced the same. It is not necessary to become absorbed in the history of intellectual theory. We can leave that to the experts. I would only like to say how successful she was as my inter-cultural interpreter on my visit to Pakistan. She frequently even opened for me the hearts of the Islamic people with whom I spoke. And it makes a difference whether one is exchanging diplomatic courtesies or, if necessary, protest messages with Presidents and government representatives or whether one succeeds in reaching beyond these traditional tools of foreign policy into the substance of relations, including their cultural substance.

However, Annemarie Schimmel's work of reconciliation is also of significance to us domestically, and we are just beginning to understand this. It is no longer possible today to separate convictions geographically. Christians, Muslims, and atheists live side by side in the same countries, in the same cities, even in the same streets and houses. In this respect, life has overtaken the dialogue between religions and cultures. However, dialogue must now follow immediately in order to ensure that living together does not turn into a nightmare. We cannot live together in the long run if we do not talk to, or know anything about, one another. With regard to Islam, Annemarie Schimmel has paved the way for us to do this, and with regard to other cultures, she has shown us how to open up such paths.

CHAPTER 3

Human Rights as a Transcultural Cause

(Essay in the Hamburg weekly Die Zeit, *6 September 1996)*[*]

THE QUESTION OF HUMAN RIGHTS and their international implementation is currently being more intensively debated in the Federal Republic of Germany than in many other countries, and that is only right. We know today that human rights form the most convincing path to peace among people, as well as among states, something the situation in Bosnia recently demonstrated once again. It is not just that there were severe infringe-

* This essay appeared as the prelude to *Die Zeit*'s much discussed series dealing with the topic of human rights.

ments of human rights there: The pressure of public opinion in Western and Islamic countries, which constituted an outflow of human rights, ensured intervention which proved an epistasis to genocide and prepared the way for the Dayton agreement. We still do not know if all of the hopes born by this agreement will be fulfilled. But one thing we do know: We at least have to try to meet them, for the sake of human rights.

In the debate on human rights, it is naturally not enough to invest available energies only in public discussions and campaigns. In this regard, good intentions do not necessarily result in good. This is especially true of the Germans, who—not on the political stage, of course, but certainly throughout society—were right there after the end of the Cold War, and the bipolarism associated with it, in searching for a global consciousness in foreign policy. One would not be completely off the mark in thinking that the discussions on human rights and their implementation throughout the world form an essential part of this national process of self-discovery, a path down which other European countries—in light of their completely different histories—have traveled much further than we.

It is especially important to avoid quick-fix alternatives, which at first seem so plausible but finally fall flat in the face of rational examination. I shall mention only three of these:

First, it is wrong that a defense of human rights only represents an intellectual exercise in favor of European ideas and, especially, that this accusation can only be countered through an absolute relativism of values.

Second, it is just as wrong to think that the only choice available is between silence in the face of human rights abuses in other countries and an infringement upon those countries' sovereignty. That might have been true until the middle of this century, but since that time we have seen the appearance of a number of human rights catalogues, and sovereignty and criticism of human rights abuses are no longer mutually exclusive.

Third, support for human rights and the maintenance of an economic relationship are not mutually exclusive either, despite the fact that the contrary is often claimed. A case might even be made for economic relationships' having an influence on human rights issues. But there are other interests besides economic ones which give rise to close relationships between particular countries—and then bring economic ties in their wake. This is especially true of the large countries of Asia and Latin America, which will play an increased geopolitical role in the next century.

These few considerations alone demonstrate that today's debate on human rights does not principally revolve around their overall right to recognition, but is centered on the question of how they can be implemented to the greatest extent possible in each particular region of the world and in each political constellation. *Whether* human rights are worthy of support is no longer the issue, but rather *how* they are to be achieved.

Our goal is the universal observation of human rights as they are prescribed in the United Nations Declaration on Human Rights of 1948 and in subsequent UN human rights documentation. No concessions can be made toward achieving this aim, and my plea here is for an unwavering stance in holding to this goal.

When its comes to realizing this aim we also have to be pragmatic. This is a word which often sounds compromising or even hypocritical to Germans. But in reality, a pragmatism which pays heed to how a rightfully acknowledged goal can be most broadly attained is everything but that, and must by no means be equated with opportunism. Politics—including the politics of human rights—is always about making genuine improvements to actual conditions, and this does not mean simply acknowledging the "courage of one's convictions" but making use of the right means at the right time.

Hitler, Pinochet, and the Greek colonels could all have been isolated by the international community, even if that had taken a great deal of effort, and that sort of approach should definitely be practiced, wherever it is possible, in the interests of human rights. But at the same time we should not forget that in other cases this is not possible. For example, how are you supposed to "isolate" a country of several hundred million people?

Whoever understands and is conscious of the fact that even the best human endeavor runs the risk of being incomplete and fallible will never dogmatically decide in favor of one side against all the others when he realizes that there are several paths to the goal, as there usually are. No, such a person will follow the precept of pragmatism and take several parallel paths.

This is nothing new. This form of pragmatism proved most successful with the former Soviet Union embodied in the human rights-oriented policies of the CSCE process (the Conference for Security and Cooperation in Europe, now the Organization for Security and Cooperation in Europe). This body incorporated the most diverse forms of interaction and endeavor: ongoing political dialogue, economic cooperation, steady support for human rights, a multiplication of forms of communication, and other confidence-building measures. The success of this approach is clear: Even if it owes a great debt of gratitude primarily to the economic collapse of the Soviet Union, it also demonstrates how much is dependant on the application of the right method to the right case.

I am well aware of the risk of being misunderstood, which is why I want to point out immediately that all of the questions and arguments which follow are in no way meant to dilute the universal application of the United Nations' human rights catalogue of 1948. Everything contained therein was reaffirmed by the 1993 Vienna Conference on Human Rights, upon which we can build.

We must, however, be allowed to pose questions concerning the implementation of the outcome of human rights policies. Who makes the decisions about whether, when, how, and where particular rights from the 1948 catalogue are put into practice?

Which forms of human rights policy involvement are suitable and appropriate for the intercourse among states? Which forms are useful? Is there a ranking or strategic list of priorities in implementing the various rights framed in the 1948 catalogue? How much leeway is there in the structural variations of individual human rights?

It would appear as though the public debate about human rights is increasingly conducted in terms of human rights as an absolute, as if their content and purview have been written in stone in Europe and are no longer in need of any further thought. But the reality of the matter is that none of the human rights catalogues which are prescribed in Western constitutions correspond completely to any other. On top of this, European states already infringe on human rights within certain limits, and differences in this regard are extensive even within Europe. To this extent, therefore, what constitutes human rights must constantly be reviewed.

For one thing, we have to be able to count on a well-defined nucleus of those human rights which are meant to spare individuals the worst infringements upon their personal integrity. Such rights include the right to respect for human life; the prohibition of serfdom, slavery, and torture; protection from arbitrary deprivation of liberty; and the prohibition of discrimination which is based on racist, religious, or similar reasons: In short, these are what are usually known as "core" human rights.

Doubt should be given no quarter when its comes to the application of these human rights throughout the world. Acknowledgement of this universality should be self-evident to us Germans. We have experienced what happens when human dignity is granted only to those members of a certain people or certain racc.

Be that as it may, our opinion on this question could take no other form one way or the other; in this regard there is no reason—consideration of the particular natures of other cultures or systems of thought notwithstanding—to make any concessions in the demand for universal application of these rights.

In particular, the widely made assertion that the roots of human rights ideology can only be found in Western culture is wrong. Real experts on the cultures of the Middle East and Asia are very well aware of the fact that the classical sources of Hinduism, Confucianism, Buddhism, and Islam erect similar standards of humanity to those of Greek antiquity, Judaism, and Christianity, upon which three traditions our culture is built. All of these cultures and their guiding philosophical systems are, in a word, based on an ethic of humanity. For example, all of them subject themselves to the Golden Rule: "Do not do unto others what you would not like them to do unto you." If this sentence alone were exercised in reality, it would cover all three of the fundamental rights I just mentioned, inasmuch as almost nobody would agree to another person's killing them, torturing them, selling them into slavery, or throwing them into jail without due process. It is clear, then, that at least the fundamental rights of humanity are a direct result of the Golden Rule, which most obviously applies in all of the world's cultures.

In the course of the debate on human rights with other peoples and cultural entities, we Europeans would be well advised to climb down from the pedestal upon which we are so fond of placing ourselves on this issue.

The process of development which we can observe today in other parts of the world, and which we so offhandedly criticize, is a process we had to go through as well, and not so long ago, it must be said.

The French Declaration of Human and Civil Rights and the first ten amendments to the United States Constitution—known as the Bill of Rights—came about in 1789 and 1791, respectively, which is to say just two hundred years ago, and their subsequent relapses are in no particular need of being highlighted. Real democracy, in which those who govern are freely elected by the governed and can be replaced, has only been around in Europe since the last century.

One of our problems lies in the fact that the course of events in other parts of the world was exactly the other way around—and still is. Only a genuine democratization can engender a gradual respect for human rights, because citizens will develop an increasing understanding of them and a corresponding demand for them. Two completely different conclusions are to be drawn in this regard:

On the one hand, it is important that democratization be seen in all parts of the world as one of the most effective strategies for achieving the implementation of human rights, and, as a consequence, we must promote that democratization.

On the other hand, under these circumstances we must also reckon with the existence of states which in all seriousness see themselves as democracies but nevertheless leave something to be desired in their realization of human rights. This may be the result of "old baggage" (having lived under the leadership of the military or police forces, sustaining a severe penal system and the like), but it may also be because the level of public consciousness on the matter has not reached the stage desirable from a Western point of view. If I interpret the matter correctly, the proper ways of dealing with such democracies—which to a certain extent still find themselves "on the road" to democracy—have not yet been fully sorted out. Of course, we can't call for the realization of human rights only after the goal of democratization has been fully achieved. But this much is true: The probability of achieving a solid human rights policy is considerably greater in these states than in those which for whatever reason have made a conscious decision against democracy and the rule of law.

It is very important that such "on the road" democracies are constantly and emphatically reminded of their shortcomings and that they be challenged to remove them. But it is also very important that these states receive the help of those democracies which have already arrived and also experience something of the trust placed in their development to democracy and the rule of law.

A part of those human rights recognized in Europe relate to economic activities. Rights in this category include the freedom to choose what work we do; the right to private property; the right to enter into contracts; the right to investment and consumption; equal access to employment, markets, and economic opportunities, including, to an extent, the right to do business wherever one wants, which was initially understood as a sort of subsidiary freedom.

All of these human rights are actually nothing more than the basic principles of the market economy or, to put it more exactly, the social market economy, if you include the possibilities of state direction and rights such as the freedom to form unions and other coalitions under the constitution.

To be sure, neither the market economy nor its constitutive human rights have so far been in a position to create a perfect and just world in all areas, and that will remain the case in the future. Nonetheless, both elements have unleashed in people a range of activity, creativity, and entrepreneurship originally unpredicted and, as a result, have made possible the leap into a completely new and—despite all the problems—better world.

There is a direct connection here between opting for human rights and making the major decision on a system, such as democracy. Many of the states in today's world whose records on human rights are far from satisfactory nevertheless declare their belief in what might more or less be described as a social market economy. But they will gradually recognize, as recognize they must, that a market economy is not possible without economic human rights. To this extent—and even if it might be repugnant to some purists—we will definitely have to get used to the idea that aid towards building up a free market–oriented society can always be an aid in the promotion of human rights. Here, too, the question is not "whether," but "how."

It may be that in some cases trade relationships may be less effective than investment, or pure European investment less effective than joint ventures. But they are all useful in terms of human rights policy, at least as a rule.

It is for this reason—and not out of some sort of thirst for economic profit—that I continue to argue for a strategy of economic exchange. I take a great deal of encouragement in this regard from the experiences of the young Asian democracies, from the Christian Philippines to Confucianist Korea and from Buddhist Thailand to Islamic Malaysia. All of these countries have shown that the birth of an economically successful and concomitantly self-confident middle class can help convert the hopes of democratic development into a real breakthrough. To reiterate the point once more: A free market presupposes at least economic freedom, and people who take advantage of this freedom and therefore achieve success will someday also demand a say in political responsibility and noneconomic freedoms. And they will preserve them.

Naturally, economic freedoms and economic development are not the only paths to human rights and democracy. For years now a Nobel Peace Prize winner in Burma has been showing us how the Buddhism-rooted expectations of the majority of her people express themselves without the positive economic developments of the region around Burma having yet taken hold in that country. But the pragmatic view can be applied here too. Where there are several paths which can be taken, as many of them as possible should be. If there is a strategy for economic development, it should be tried.

The major difficulties found in international discourse arise from a third group of human rights, which I shall summarize here under the heading "freedom of thought" and which includes such rights as freedom of the media, freedom of learning, and freedom of artistic expression. For us Europeans, all of these rights are quite simply inalienable. We are especially aware of the fact that without these rights our entire political and intellectual culture, as well as our knowledge of the physical world, society, and the humanities, would not exist. But it is on exactly this point that we continually come across problems in seeing eye to eye with our global interlocutors.

Unless we are very much mistaken, we stand today at the beginning of a new geopolitical era. Cultures and philosophies which were, until recently, still suppressed or somehow disenfranchised, are awaking to a new self-confidence, and diverse views of humankind and the world are also beginning to run up against each other in international politics: I repeat the previously given examples of Buddhism, Islam, and Confucianism.

There is another aspect to all of this: The more independent the peoples of the former "third" world become, the more they will recognize their own worth, and search for their own identities. In the process, many of these peoples are still having to liberate themselves from the injury and offense caused by long years of colonial imposition while simultaneously fighting an often hopeless battle for food and the most primitive provisions of water, living space, health care, and education. This is why meeting such basic needs—which are ultimately the basis of all human rights—is to be given absolute priority over all other human rights considerations.

Those who wish to promote international rights have to be constantly aware of this issue; even then it will be extremely difficult, both in terms of dialogue and in dealing with the conception upon which one's own political remedies are based. The right to freely express one's opinion is perforce of less significance to a hungry person than to one who is full.

Pari passu the concept of the rights of the individual will be of less interest to an African still living in the tradition of his tribe than to a member of individualistic Western society. And it is not very easy for a Chinese who grew up with the ethic of duty found in Confucianism to understand why we are so fond of putting rights at the forefront of things.

Neither should we close our eyes to the fact that even in countries with well-established social structures there can be social disquiet which leads to demands for human rights and democracy. Even those cultures which traditionally place duties above rights were never monolithic collectives, and won't be in the future. Here, too, there are people who are capable of free thought and desire to exercise it. Should such people be subjected to persecution and threats on their lives, nobody can view such a state of affairs with equanimity.

It has been my experience that scientific research provides excellent help for the argument in this dialogue, inasmuch as such research finds itself right in the line between freedom of thought and freedom of commerce. This is because an economy without effective—which is to say, free—research and the free transference of research results is, in the long run, condemned to death. Even the most rigorous skeptics on human rights can see this is true of one explains it to them clearly enough. Freedom of knowledge, therefore, can build a bridge to all the other forms of freedom of thought, even if that bridge is often a narrow one.

Human rights engender demands on states and societies, and when we Germans press others to observe and implement human rights we are making demands, whether we intend to or not, on them politically. If that is the case, then our co-dialogists can also expect that we take their concrete situations into account, and I have my doubts as to whether we do this adequately.

Of course there can be no compromising when it comes to the fundamental rights of the person—life, liberty, protection from slavery and arbitrary deprivation of liberty, and protection from discrimination. No political or social order can justify infringements upon such rights.

But what about related issues which are not core ideas in human rights? In our discussions up until now, have we, for example, taken enough account of how very much, in some regions of the world, the fight to survive has determined the place of the person in the family or other groups? Can we really demand of such people that their personal priorities should be oriented along our Western, individualistic lines?

And do we really know what it is like for a country to have to feed and support 900 million or even 1.2 billion people? In such circumstances can we really hold China's one-child policy up to our standards? Can we be critical of restrictions on population movement in heavily populated countries, even though they are intended to prevent migration and more slums in the city, which also represent violations of human dignity? In our own case, we begin to panic about competition for jobs and being swamped by foreigners when we are confronted with the immigration of a few hundred thousand southern and eastern Europeans!

We do not have any panacea, either, as to how the rapid economic development and fundamental structural changes taking place in, say, Russia are to be handled without any social missteps. We have been experiencing enough difficulties with the comparatively "simple" case of our new federal states.

I am therefore asking for the greatest care to be taken even in the very phrasing of our human rights policy. There can be no relativism in the area of core human rights, as already noted. But above and beyond those, every problem has to be looked at and evaluated individually, and account has to be taken of the cultural and developmental particularities of the country concerned.

But we have to make sure that any political measures to be taken, including their suitability, are aimed at the right people and at the right time.

It is most important that we take things on a case-by-case basis in deciding whether to pursue avenues of gentle persuasion, on the one hand, or sanctions, on the other.

All things being equal, countries which are making serious efforts toward democracy usually deserve the more gentle form of argumentation. In these cases, political commonalities are generally so many that they form an excellent basis for demanding human rights. Such countries' desire for closer contacts with international communities which subscribe to liberal democracy (the North Atlantic Treaty Organization, the European Union, and so on) also acts as an impetus in bringing about human rights.

In the case of those countries which consciously are not moving in the direction of democracy and the rule of law, the experience of the Conference for Security and Cooperation in Europe calls for something other than an exclusively conflictual approach. Of course this should not be discounted out of hand either, especially when it comes to those countries where it might offer some success. But even here we should not completely renege on patient "nagging," and we certainly should not damn this approach as weak, hypocritical, or opportunist.

During the days of the CSCE, the Soviet Union was not prepared to discuss its internal human rights situation. A breakdown in relations would at that time have had grave consequences for the West inasmuch as it would naturally have brought about a termination of all disarmament negotiations. It was a much better strategy, therefore, to maintain the relationship and transfer the problem of human rights to the multinational and transnational level, for example to the CSCE.

Moreover, there was increasingly a policy of contact on the nongovernment level. Even before the end of the Cold War, such diverse and decentralized contacts supported the rise of independent types of citizens' groups which would later be of valuable help in the transition to the first stages of democracy. The number of examples (Poland, Hungary, Czechoslovakia) shows that such action could also be effective in other parts of the world.

I would like to reiterate once more the fact that the same approach will not be successful with all states. We are today well aware of the fact that the economic sanctions imposed upon South Africa by the United States of America played a considerable role in the downfall of the system of apartheid. Similar sanctions at that time against the Soviet Union would have remained unrealistic and were, therefore, never even tried. In this light, the oft-heard alternative "human rights or Western greed for profits" is, as these two examples clearly show, much too simplistic. There have been cases in which the break-off of economic—and diplomatic—relations has proven a courageous yet simultaneously ineffective measure, one which dashes all hopes of a switch to cooperation.

There is no doubt that there will always be much argument about which methods in which case and, particularly, at which time will be the correct ones, in terms of the success they promise. This debate ought to be carried out in a sober and realistic fashion. Realism and idealism, policies of interest and policies of responsibility, are not mutually exclusive. To the extent that it was not wrong to talk to the Soviet Union about all things, including security policy, then, equally, it cannot be wrong—in commercial intercourse with Asian countries—to keep an eye on the security of German jobs as well as human rights.

And there is one thing that simply cannot be denied: Each and every policy which may be pursued regarding these issues may someday prove to be wrong, in part or in whole.

CHAPTER 4

Asia and the West

(Excerpts from a speech given at a dinner in honor of His Excellency Mr. Jiang Zemin, President of the People's Republic of China, Schloss Augustusburg, 13 July 1995)

[. . .] EUROPE'S INTEREST IN CHINA dates back exactly 700 years. Following Marco Polo's return from his voyage to the Middle Kingdom in 1295, China became for Europeans a source of cultural fascination, a beacon of scientific discovery, and a magnet for economic interests. One would be hard put to find in the history of mankind a more impressive and enduring example of such an attraction between cultures.

This vivid mutual interest should not come as a surprise, however. One only need bear in mind that both Europeans and Chinese began to ask themselves, almost simultaneously, but quite independently of one another, the same questions, not a mere 700 years ago, but as many as 2,500 years ago. We forget all too often that Confucius and Socrates lived in the same century. Though they knew nothing of each other's existence, they both concerned themselves with the same humanity, the same reason, the same pursuit of knowledge, the same dichotomy between good and evil, the same need to vanquish injustice and violence.

It has become fashionable these days to speak of the "clash of civilizations" as the next great confrontation after the Cold War. I, for one, am of the opinion that the political leaders should see to it that this scenario does not become a self-fulfilling prophecy. And this is why, last January, I recalled in a speech in Davos the Golden Rule that is to be found in Confucius's teachings as well as in the Bible, in Buddhist sutras as well as in the traditions of Hinduism: "Do not do unto others what you would not like them to do unto you." I was delighted to hear that the foreign minister of the People's Republic of China cited that very same rule at a conference in Beijing in May.

Like Confucius, Aristotle distinguished between law and ethics. While in our Western tradition the law and, with it, civil liberties assumed ever-greater significance, in the Confucian tradition it was ethics and thus civic responsibilities which prevailed. From my own professional experience, I cannot but wish that our two cultures move towards a point of equilibrium between those two traditions—our different ways of life notwithstanding. Both Aristotle and Confucius, were they still alive today, would no doubt strongly recommend that we pursue such a course. For they were both advocates of the "right mean" for solving the problems of mankind, including those of a political nature.

On reflection, we know a great deal about one another. For decades, mutual academic research and teaching has been going on in our two countries—in Germany about China, in China about Germany. Chinese is taught at German universities, German at Chinese universities.

I was even told that you, Mr. President, can recite, in German, verses from one of Goethe's poems. And it is in Goethe's very work that we find the most appropriate response to your interest in

German literature. Goethe scholars have drawn my attention to one of his poems, which, through the medium of language, evokes in the mind's eye a scenic Chinese countryside at dusk. It so befits the evening which we are spending together that I took the liberty of having a copy of it placed next to your cover.

Meanwhile, the number of students and scientists exchanged between our two countries goes into the thousands. Modern electronic systems disseminate within seconds a large amount of information in both directions, and in our newspapers we can regularly read about one another. Every day planes carry hundreds of businessmen and tourists from China to Germany and vice versa. We are becoming closer and learning ever more from each other.

And hence we also know that our views still diverge markedly on an issue each of our two countries considers crucial. I refer to the relationship between the individual, on the one hand, and society (i.e. the state), on the other. No one will dispute that there is room for earnest discussions on this subject. For instance, at what point should individual rights yield to society's rights, and when do the latter begin to infringe on the former? What means do we afford each side for asserting and defending its respective rights? And to what extent are these rights guaranteed?

A dialogue on these issues has begun. And it can be carried on in the spirit of those traditions I mentioned earlier. Our common goal must be to strike a consensual balance between individual rights and those of the state. And although such a balance cannot be set identically in every country on earth, it may neither be so weighted against the individual as to harm him or her, nor so tilted against society as to destabilize it. At any rate, our experience of the last decades in the Federal Republic has taught us this: Society is most stable when both the participation of each and every citizen in the decision-making process of the state and his or her individual freedoms are guaranteed by laws that are truly enforceable. [. . .]

(Excerpts from a speech on the occasion of being awarded an honorary degree by the Faculty of Law of Waseda University, Tokyo, 7 April 1997)

[. . .] There is one problem in the foreign-policy domain which is perhaps a particular challenge to Germany and Japan, a conceptual and cultural challenge. I am thinking here of the so-called clash of civilizations which, following the Cold War, some people predict as the next great conflict looming on the horizon. This scenario is to my mind highly questionable both intellectually and morally. But it is nonetheless highly dangerous. For this idea, once implanted in the minds of the elites both in the West and in Asia, might become a self-fulfilling prophecy, hence a new security risk. I am convinced, however, that Japan and Germany are well equipped historically and intellectually to ensure that this scenario never becomes a reality.

This brings me to an argument in favor of Germans and Japanese's being partners in responsibility, namely, our wealth of shared values and historical experience. After all, it is not the first time that the German and the Japanese people find themselves facing tremendous challenges. And reflecting on our problems as we approach the twenty-first century, we would do well to recall the sources of moral and intellectual strength which in the past have helped us find a sense of direction in times of uncertainty, solve problems, correct mistakes, and evoke visions for the future.

When I speak of shared values and experience, I am not just referring to the 400 years of reciprocal cultural fascination dating back to the arrival in Japan of the Jesuit Francis Xavier in 1549. That story has been recounted often enough, so I'm not going to repeat it here. However, if we look back for a moment at the unforgettable part played therein by travelling scholars like

Engelbert Kämpfer, poets like Goethe, physicians like Philipp-Franz von Siebold, statesmen and reformers like Ito Hirobumi, lawyers like Heinrich Rössler, heroes of the heart like Mori Ogai, and prisoners of war like the music-makers of Bando, or again physicists like Einstein and philanthropic industrialists like Hajime Hoshi, all this seems to point to a very special affinity between Japan and Germany. And the very depth of this affinity should preserve us, I believe, from making hasty judgements postulating a clash of civilizations stemming from some innate contradiction between Asian and Western values.

Considering how important this point is for both our countries, allow me to go one step further. Even more striking than our fascination for each other's cultures over the past 400 years are the common foundations of our civilizations reaching back into the distant past, when we never even knew of each other's existence, and later on, when contacts were nonexistent. We all too easily forget, for instance, that Buddha, Confucius, and Socrates were virtual contemporaries, all bent on the same quest for humanity, reason, wisdom, and distinguishing good from evil. My response to the clash-of-civilizations school of thought is to insist on the Golden Rule, which is formulated in almost identical terms both in the writings of Confucius and in the Bible, and indeed in some form or other in all great civilizations "Do not do unto others what you would not like them to do unto you." Of course I know there are many different religions, philosophies, and traditions in this pluralistic world of ours, and it is only natural and right that in times of change and upheaval people feel the urge to go back to their own ethical roots. But that surely need not mean that, grappling as we are with the same problems, we must at the present juncture go divergent ways, with possibly hazardous implications!

If this were so, then how could Japan, I wonder, become a model of a consensual society? For does not Japan's culture rest on the three pillars of Shintoism, Buddhism and Confucianism, which together form a happy and harmonious whole? One of the reasons I have been looking forward to this visit with such keen interest is, I will readily admit, to experience at first hand this remarkable Japanese cultural harmony. Peaceful and creative dialogue between different religions and philosophies is, I believe, one of the most challenging tasks facing us today, and as far as I am concerned, those prophets of the looming clash of civilizations should take the trouble to study the Japanese example of pragmatic tolerance.

Apart from the common ethical foundations of Western and Asian civilization, I am struck also by certain similarities of a historical nature. We can trace comparable patterns of transition from the old to the new, progress and setbacks, paralysis and renewal in the history of both Japan and Germany. Take the adoption and simultaneous adaptation of Roman traditions in Germany and Chinese traditions in Japan in the early Middle Ages. Take medieval feudalism, which was unique to Europe and Japan and gave way to a vibrant mercantile society featuring almost-modern commodity and financial markets both in Osaka and the Free Imperial Cities of the Holy Roman Empire. Take, finally, the mathematician Kowa Seki who, in the Japan of self-imposed isolation of the Tokugawa Period, discovered some of the same theorems of calculus as his contemporaries Leibniz and Newton.

From the perspective of the nineteenth century, the Germany of the Humboldt reforms and the Japan of the Meiji Restoration seem to have been destined for partnership. The ups and downs of the remarkably similar history of Germany and Japan in the twentieth century need no elaboration. We are all familiar with them. The wars and the failure of democracy in the first half of this century hold a message we should never forget. But when we focus on the miracle of reconstruction, the success of our democracies in the second half, the message is one of encouragement and hope.

This brief expedition through time shows that the links between the classical sources and history of our cultures to the present day and beyond are easily found. And that brings me to a further argument in favor of Germans and Japanese being partners in responsibility: our obvious interest in evolving common perspectives for the future.

It seems to me we are already hard at work developing such new perspectives, even if the climate of the ongoing public debate is for the moment one of gloom and self-doubt. We are at any rate already discussing ways of tackling the problems besetting the economy, society, culture, and foreign relations. And just as the analysis of the problems is similar, so too is there a lot of common ground in our approaches to a solution.

In both countries we are increasingly realizing that globalization is here to stay, and there is no alternative but to make the best of it. We are beginning to understand that this cannot be done without deregulating the economy and mobilizing all groups and creative forces in our society. This does not mean pinning our hopes on some new form of social Darwinism, or submitting to the law of the survival of the fittest. The search for consensus, which has been such a consistent theme of the past 50 years in both Germany and Japan, is not something we should give up lightly. The Golden Rule I cited earlier is still the benchmark of a humane society and a guide to decision-making in both the private and the public domain.

This must also be our focus in dealing with the demographic problem. If we do nothing and let the shrinking number of young people bear the burden of caring for the growing number of elderly people, their prospects for the future will be blighted. Yet we owe it to the older generation, who built up a country devastated by war, not to abandon them in the sunset of their lives. This is a classic case for the Golden Rule. Static models offer no solution. Redistribution or saving alone cannot be the answer. Nor can it be found in conventional patterns of growth based on fiscal expansion. Our difficult budgetary situation leaves no scope for such policies.

What we need is a new type of growth, knowledge-based growth, in fact. As we approach the twenty-first century, our countries are on the threshold of a new era, much as was Germany at the time of the Humboldt reforms or Japan at the time of the Meiji Restoration. Once more we have to make a massive investment in research and education. The ecological and fiscal limits to conventional growth are a straightjacket from which we can only escape by developing what is called our human capital. Knowledge knows no limits. The law of diminishing returns does not apply to investment in brains.

All of this can happen if we want it to happen. Japan's vision of a microelectronic revolution, which it saw through, despite much resistance, to a triumphant success within a decade, still fills us Germans with admiration. This kind of pragmatic strategy is also what we need to solve our current problems. The crux of the matter is to combine forward-looking action with an awareness of the fallibility of human understanding and a readiness at any time to correct decisions which turn out to be wrong. The new dynamism evident in the American economy, science, and technology is proof that today this can still be done. We should remember that at the end of the eighties the United States, too, was prey to that mood of despondency which is so pervasive in Japan and Germany today. Let that spur us to shake off our current depression and turn our thoughts to shaping the future of our economy, society, and culture.

Globalization and information technology are in fact giving us a new type of sovereignty which we are still just learning how to use. We need to ask whether we are making sufficient use or indeed the right use of it. Above all we need to recognize we cannot make full and wise use of technical progress unless on the intellectual, mental, and cultural plane we are always one stride ahead.

This also means, of course, that we must invest in foreign-policy know-how as well if Germany and Japan are to live up to their growing international responsibilities. For in the final analysis the skills needed for the exercise of "soft power" are derived from the richness of our scientific potential and cultural traditions. One key to developing such power in the long term lies in a far-sighted education policy geared to the needs of the twenty-first century.

But another key, we would do well to remember, lies in our own history, our wealth of experience from ancient times right up to this century. The Golden Rule I would cite one last time is more relevant than ever before for foreign policy. I can conceive of no more powerful rebuttal of the clash-of-civilizations thesis. I was delighted to learn, as a matter of fact, that the Chinese foreign minister quoted the Confucian version of the Golden Rule at a conference in Beijing in May 1995. To live by this rule means we must be good neighbors to one another within both Asia and Europe. What's more, Asia and Europe must be good neighbors to each other. For Germany and Japan this opens up a whole range of opportunities for responsibility in partnership. They can make it their highest priority to demonstrate in political practice what it means to be a good neighbor and inspire others to follow their example.

In the history of relations between our two countries there have been periods of intensive German learning from Japan and intensive Japanese learning from Germany. Now as we look to the future we have a chance to at the same time learn from each other, which also means learning from our mistakes. If we succeed we will be helping to create a global environment favorable to learning, in short, a learning world. As to the goal of this learning, there can be no doubt. At the dawn of this new century it is nothing less than to construct a more humane world.

CHAPTER 5

Towards a Universal Civilization

(Excepts from a speech prior to the lectures on the topic "Towards a universal civilization" at the Institute of Islamic Understanding [IKIM], Kuala Lumpur, 3 April 1997)

I HAVE BEEN TOLD that the Institute of Islamic Understanding is the first and only body of its kind striving to promote cultural understanding in two ways—by increasing knowledge and fostering mutual comprehension—and is thus particularly keen to enter into a dialogue with representatives of other religions and cultures.

You have devoted yourself and your Institute to the dialogue between cultures, an issue which I consider to be one of the most important of our time, one which inevitably unites Asia and Europe.

The end of the Cold War by no means brought about the end of history. On the one hand, the globalization of markets, technology, the media, even interactive societies seems to be unstoppable. On the other hand, we have witnessed time and again, even in seemingly enlightened societies, the tendency to relapse into a national or cultural drawbridge mentality, thinking in terms of power, and the evocation of enemy-images. The fashionable "clash of civilizations" scenario, which predicts that the Cold War will be succeeded by global cultural conflict, is a typical example of this way of thinking. I regard this scenario as academically and ethically questionable. However, if it is disseminated by the media and becomes established in the minds of the elites it could easily become a self-fulfilling prophecy.

America, Asia, and Europe have an equal interest, even in terms of security policy, in combating the intellectual fallacies of this scenario. Institutes such as yours and events such as today's can make an important contribution towards this.

The theme of today's event, namely the question as to whether a universal civilization is conceivable, plays a central role in efforts to achieve inter-cultural harmony. As we all know, Professor Huntington rejects this possibility out of hand. That is why his scenario is so dangerous. Does not civilization all over the world at the very least mean preserving peace, controlling aggression, seeking knowledge? Do we realize what we are unleashing if we abandon the idea of a minimum degree of common civilization?

Of course there are several major religions and a host of cultures in the world. But how can one seriously doubt that they are all concerned with civilizing humanity? I am always reminding Western advocates of the cultural clash scenario, by way of example, that 700 years ago there was a major Islamic enlightenment while Christian Europe was paralyzed by medieval dogma. Those who prefer modern examples can read in textbooks, for instance, that the concept of a zero, without which our decimal system and the binary system used in computer science would be inconceivable, came to Western mathematics from Hindu culture via Islamic culture. Can mathematics be regarded as anything but a part of universal civilization?

(Excerpts from a speech at the State Banquet Hosted by His Majesty Tuanku Ja'afar Ibn Al-Marhum Tuanku Abdul Rahman, Yang di Pertuan Agong of Malaysia, 1 April 1997)

[. . .] Malaysia is becoming increasingly important, not only in Asia but also in the global debate on the prospects for the twenty-first century. The astounding dynamism of Malaysia's economy, the creativity and confidence of its people are linked with a deep awareness of your country's cultural values. Just as a tree or bush cannot survive without roots, people cannot prosper if they do not become conscious of their cultural heritage and are thus able to determine their position in the present.

Malaysia stands out because people from quite different cultural, religious, societal, and economic spheres live here peacefully and form a harmonious community. Your country is an example of the dialogue between cultures from which Europe can, and indeed should, learn. [. . .]

Let me emphasize that the dialogue between cultures and religions is one of the primary tasks of our age. This particularly applies to relations between Christianity and Islam. I would like to think that together Germany and Malaysia can help prevent a worldwide "clash of cultures," which is unfortunately a fashionable idea at the moment, and instead contribute to the creation of a universal civilization in which all cultures can develop to their fullest extent. [. . .]

CHAPTER 6

Cultures, Economics, and Democracy

(Speech to the Federation of Korean Industry [FKI], Seoul, 17 September 1998)

THE UNIQUE AFFINITY BETWEEN OUR TWO COUNTRIES we owe not only to our shared experience as divided nations but also to an astounding number of other features we have in common.

At the same time, however, Germany is part of Europe and Korea part of Asia, both regions currently caught up in a vortex of change. Both are challenged as never before to work together as partners. I am bound therefore to speak from a European perspective as well—and for a European, as I hope to show, Korea affords a particularly good perspective from which to observe what is happening in Asia.

But it is not just in Asia and Europe that a sea change is taking place. The globalization phenomenon has the whole world in its grip, sowing seeds of change in nations and cultures, economies and societies. Since Germany and Korea, Europe and Asia are all equally affected, allow me, too, to make here a few comments of my own.

Let me start with the process of transformation we are currently seeing in Europe and Asia.

In Europe, after much heated debate, the launch of the euro has been decided. With the markets now convinced of its success, "Euroland" is proving a kind of safe haven in the light of the turbulence affecting currencies in Asia, Latin America, and Russia. Perhaps this experience will be seen in the longer term as a useful trial run for East Asia.

However, for European industry the really tough structural adjustments still lie in the future. Monetary union and enlargement to the east will radically transform the European Union. In the single market both will accelerate the pace of economic change and make also for fiercer competition. Disparities in regional development will be revealed, and the spotlight turned on inefficient institutions and uncompetitive companies. Eastern enlargement will also force us to reform the institutions of the Union. In the emerging market countries of Eastern Europe, too, enormous changes will be required in the political and economic domain as well as in the way people think and act, if their accession to the Union is to be a success.

At the same time Asia is in the throes of an economic crisis that, sparked off by a seemingly isolated problem in Thailand, then spread to the whole of East and South-East Asia, is now on the point of engulfing Latin America and Russia and may be threatening the entire world economy. The Asian crisis has set a process of restructuring in train on a scale that seems for the moment even more formidable than that taking place in Europe and which for some may indeed obscure the long-term perspective.

Considering that not so long ago the amazing boom in East and South-East Asia was described as the Asian miracle, it is strange indeed that the gurus of our time have identified a "typically Asian" crisis. The talk now is all of an Asian failure rather than an Asian miracle. I for my part believe both these views are clichés and therefore wrong.

For all the current turmoil, we should not lose sight of one fundamental fact: In the years ahead there will be no decline in East and South-East Asia's key role in international affairs and the world economy. After all, Asian growth was not some kind of monetary and financial bubble but the product of the real economy. This was due above all to a highly educated population, a readiness to embrace technological progress, and an extraordinary entrepreneurial dynamism. These qualities have not gone by the board.

Another point I would make is that all the media hype we hear at times about some kind of opposition between Western and Asian economic cultures results in more damage than useful insights or actual solutions to problems. There is no such thing as "European" mathematics, "American" theories of civilization, or "Asian" economics, for that matter. Any scientific theory worth its salt is universal, like the laws of mathematics and logic. The fact is that the economic and monetary crisis in Asia is not a crisis of culture but a debt crisis, and debt crises are manageable, provided a responsible international economic policy is adopted as was the case with the Mexican debt crisis, for example. Such crises become dangerous in the extreme only when lack of timely action results in a drift to depression, as happened in the world economic crisis that occurred 70 years ago.

Of course the crisis in Asia is also related to the fact that some of its markets were—at least partially—cut off from world markets; that we should not forget. But first and foremost the crisis is a crisis of confidence in the international capital markets. American and European funds, once so enthusiastic about the Asian tigers' dizzying growth, suddenly rushed into headlong flight. Both reactions were in fact exaggerated. Alan Greenspan, the Chairman of the Federal Reserve Board, rightly criticized "irrational exuberance" in the markets. The same goes, however, for the opposite. Depression, too, is irrational, and this I mean as a warning to leaders not only in Asia but also in America and Europe.

What is needed now is to calm these erratic swings, to restore and stabilize some equilibrium. Here the Asian countries themselves can make a decisive contribution, by improving their banking supervision and regulation of capital markets, and especially by strengthening democratic structures. It is evidently no coincidence that Korea, a functioning democracy, is doing far better than certain others in overcoming the crisis.

I am particularly happy to be able to say this here in Korea. The example of Korean democracy clearly gives the lie to the cliché view much in vogue until not so long ago: In Asia, it was asserted, the clocks ticked differently and Confucianism would inevitably produce radically different social and political systems than elsewhere. Of course it goes without saying that different cultural and historical experiences leave their own stamp on society. Yet no one today could have any grounds for claiming that democracy is unfit for Asia or indeed that democracy is unfit as such.

President Kim Dae Jung himself in an article arousing worldwide interest has pointed out that democratic thought is grounded in Asian philosophy, too. He recalled that in the heartland of Confucianism, China, the philosopher Mencius postulated the sovereign's dependence on the will of the people just at the same time as this concept was developing in classical Greece. Similar democratic antecedents he identified in Buddhism and nineteenth-century Korean Tonghak philosophy.

The breakthrough of democratic ideas we witnessed in southern Europe in the seventies and have seen since the mid-eighties in Asia and Latin America and finally since 1989 in Eastern Europe is by far the most significant international development of recent years. While there is no automatic link, it has tended to run parallel with the worldwide trend towards the market economy, the second dimension of an open society. I for one am convinced that we are still a long way from the end of this triumphant march of democracy and the market economy.

What is behind this triumph of the open society? Political scientists could fill volumes explaining the reasons but I will confine myself to just five. The first is that people of all cultures naturally want a stake in the political life of society and a share in its prosperity. The most direct access to the former is democracy, to the latter the market economy.

But the open society is not just a response to the natural striving for freedom and self-fulfillment that is found in all cultures. It also—and here I come to my second reason—has a functional advantage over other models of society: I am thinking here of the principle of competition, and more particularly the competition of ideas. This is what makes both democracy and the market economy institutionalized processes of discovery, so to speak. Democracy is a quest for the best solutions to political problems, while the market economy is about finding the best products at the lowest possible prices.

The principle of competition definitely does not mean there can be no solidarity or voluntary cooperation in society. I know that close collaboration between government and the banking and business sector as practiced in Asia is often criticized by Western observers as corporatism. But here, too, I think we should avoid generalizations. In Germany as well, in Europe and even in America various forms of cooperation and partnership exist between important public and private economic players. Such cooperation has certainly borne fruit in Germany, for example, where both sides of industry have been willing to compromise in collective bargaining and avoid industrial conflict. In America cooperation between government and the private sector has helped promote long-term development strategies in the microelectronics sector. However, close cooperation between government and business also carries the risk that dysfunctional developments tend to be obscured or covered up. Nor does it function well unless there is also a social dimension, with employees as well having a strong voice and representation.

Let me state as the fourth advantage of an open society the principle of the free flow of information. This ensures that people are aware and can make use of the early warning systems and problem-solving mechanisms available at all different levels of political and economic life.

My fifth reason, the principle of academic freedom, I believe is for the open society a particularly valuable asset. Academic and scientific research holds not just the key to the pace of innovation in the economy and hence the well-being and social security of our citizens. Also in tackling the immense challenges of our time, such as responding to changes in the global climate or feeding the world's population, it is vital that we have access to the best research results from all over the world.

In that watershed year of 1989 the former Eastern bloc yielded peacefully to these five overwhelming advantages of an open society. Especially in times of upheaval, such as now, no one can have any interest in jettisoning them, neither in Asia nor Europe nor Russia.

That the crisis is viewed by experts in Germany as a restructuring process and that there will certainly be neither a mass departure from Asia nor a loss of confidence in Korean democracy is, by the way, obvious from the size of the German business delegation present here today.

So it is with great optimism that I turn now to my second subject: the state of German-Korean relations. Among the present company are representatives of German firms that even in this hour of crisis have decided to invest heavily in Korea. Such entrepreneurial decisions say more about our continued high esteem for your country than any amount of words. And they show, too, that Korea has friends in Germany who are friends in need and therefore friends indeed.

That is no wonder, considering all our two nations have in common still today:

- There is the long-standing fascination for each other's cultures.
- There are the surprising affinities in outlook and behavior. We Germans, for instance, are reminded by the typically Korean virtues of hard work and dependability of some of the better Prussian traditions.
- There is the fact that as countries lacking in natural resources we have both had to become exporting nations.
- There are the particularly intensive and lively contacts in arts and sciences.
- There are the 30,000 Koreans living and working in our country who are much appreciated and respected by the German public.
- And there is, finally, our shared experience as divided nations.

As President of a reunited Germany I would like to say this to all Koreans: Reunification as well will one day be one more shared experience of our two nations.

In the long run maintaining unnatural divisions through the heart of a nation is impossible; that has been proved by the German experience. It may not be possible to foresee how and when reunification will take place. But that it will happen can hardly be doubted.

Let me, however, also say this: When that historic opportunity arose, Germany found itself completely unprepared. Korea fortunately will have more time to prepare for that day, as for eight years now it has been able to observe and learn from the German experience.

In this forum I would like to point to just some of these lessons that one day might also be of value to Korea:

- The pace of change must be tempered so people are not overwhelmed. People living for decades under the thumb of an authoritarian state need time to come to terms with the new realities. I have immense admiration for the way our citizens in Eastern Germany have adapted. However, many have been left almost in a state of shock by the scale of the changes taking place in every area of life. That is why it was and still is vital to explain this new order of society and what the values are on which it is built.
- The process of transforming an internationally uncompetitive command economy into a modern market economy inevitably means unproductive jobs will be lost and many skills no longer needed. Rebuilding the economy and giving people new skills will therefore require time and patience—as well as solidarity and help across the erstwhile border.
- Reunification is indeed a new beginning, yet it is important to avoid blanket condemnations or suggestions that everything in people's past lives was worthless. No dictatorship is just that and nothing else—and in a dictatorship millions of decent citizens still have to live their lives and try to make the best of their difficult situation. That is important for people to remember, on whichever side of the old border they lived. It is clearly crucial, then, that people in both parts of the reunited country should learn about each other's past experiences. Even then the scars of the decades-long division will continue to be seen and felt for years to come.

Yet however onerous the burden of transformation may seem, whatever doubts, experiences, and advice may be evoked, when the defining moment comes, when reunification is within your grasp, there is only one thing to do: Seize that chance, do not hesitate!

Thanks to their particular experiences Germany and Korea have in some respects become models for other countries in their regions. But now, as the next millennium dawns, new challenges, new visions for the twenty-first century, the globalization era, lie ahead. Asia and Europe should meet these challenges together. The greater the turmoil, I might even say disorder, in the world, the more urgent it is that all those in positions of responsibility should subscribe to clear maxims that can provide reliable bearings for the next millennium and prevent worst-case scenarios. To six such maxims I would invite your particular attention:

Firstly, let us pledge to renounce nationalism, the arms race, and power politics. A repetition in Asia of Europe's historic mistakes would be catastrophic not just for the region but for the whole world.

My second maxim: Having just ended the ideological confrontation of the Cold War, let us not now espouse new scenarios of cultural and religious confrontation, as if humanity could not do without the law of the jungle even for a while. Obviously these days, whether in Europe, America, or other parts of the world, outbreaks of fundamentalist violence claiming some kind of cultural or religious justification are a daily occurrence. Yet on closer study it is clear the people behind such violence are all ultimately bent on destroying their own society and culture.

From a historical perspective, by the way, it seems to me that the classical sources of the world's great cultures and religions are generally more "enlightened," if I may put it that way, than later dogmas and myths. After all, they usually began as movements of renewal. Our contemporary view of Christianity, Islam, Buddhism, or Confucianism should therefore not be determined by the ideological distortions later propagated by ultra-orthodoxy. In reality, the rich variety of cultural traditions in the world can be a source of strength. I know no better proof of this than the harmonious modus vivendi in present-day Korea between Confucianism, Buddhism, and Christianity.

With my third maxim I want to urge that in today's global economy we eschew "beggar-thy-neighbor" policies, competitive devaluations, social dumping, and protectionism. Such policies would send the global economy into a downward spiral that can only end in the kind of world depression that occurred 70 years ago. And allowing a depression to happen, as I said before, would be irrational in the extreme.

The three maxims I have expounded so far have been about what not to do. Now I will add three that in the coming century offer positive strategies for constructive cooperation between Europe and Asia.

Fourthly, then, we should pursue an active communication strategy as a means of building confidence. With the CSCE, a process of communication across ideological and geographical frontiers, Europe achieved a historic breakthrough that ultimately overcame the division of Europe and of Germany. That is a strategy which can be repeated anywhere in the world.

As my fifth maxim I propose a global and inter-cultural learning and research strategy aimed at identifying and implementing solutions to concrete problems. We need a global learning and research community if we are to respond to the global nature of the immense challenges of the present day. Think of the stabilization of the world economy, the need to restore an ecological balance, the fight against international organized crime. Or another common concern, the area of peacekeeping, conflict prevention, and settlement of disputes. Political leadership is essential, especially to explain to people back home why they and their countries are affected by global issues seemingly so far removed from their lives. In its embrace of democracy and vigorous efforts to overcome the economic crisis Korea has shown just such leadership qualities.

As my sixth and final maxim I would call for better use of the existing mechanisms of international and interregional cooperation. In the Asia-Pacific region APEC is already a very good start towards the goal of enhanced cooperation. Another encouraging development worth pursuing further is the Europe/Asia cooperation at the ASEM summits. That is the right way forward. However, cooperation does not have to be confined to the level of intergovernmental organizations. It is important that this level can build on the broadest possible network of contacts in all spheres of society. Only through contacts between citizens can a universal civil society emerge, and this is exactly what the twenty-first century will need.

These six maxims sum up, I feel, the most important lessons for the new century we can draw from Asian and European experiences. Our changing contemporary world is headed in the direction of global systems—and not just in the economic domain. Cultures, societies, and individuals are in ever-closer contact, while of course maintaining their distinct cultural identity. Particularly when the going is tough we also need intensive inter-cultural and people-to-people contact and dialogue.

Of one thing, at any rate, I am today firmly convinced: In the twenty-first century Europe and Asia are ideal partners for such cooperation.

CHAPTER 7

Maxims of Responsibility in a Globalized World

(Opening address at the World Economic Forum, Davos, on 28 January 1999)

THE FINAL COUNTDOWN TO THE TWENTY-FIRST CENTURY has started. When I spoke before this Forum in 1995, the theme was still that of globalization. We are now already speaking of "globality." The process has become a state. Globalization is shaping the transition into the next century. Its effects are evident in politics, the economy, culture, and society.

You will be dealing over the next few days with the tension between globality and responsibility. I expect that your emphasis will be on the consequences of economic globality, as would be natural at a World Economic Forum. After all, many of the drastic changes which the world is undergoing have economic aspects, economic motives, or economic effects—technical breakthroughs, the industrial revolution towards the information society, the global integration of markets, and competition of locations for investment.

If, however, capital and investment focus too much on chasing factor prices around the world, what, if anything, is left for politics, society, and culture? Will they be dwarfed by global economic processes? Will politics degenerate into a mere repair shop for economic developments which are damaging in human or social terms? If this were the case, globality would have robbed politics of its essence: its orientation towards people, who stand at the center of, and define, any community. Globality forces us to seek not only a new economic and financial order, but also a worldwide social order. How can people reconquer center stage? Is it possible to turn around the pressure to conform, which globality exercises on politics, and to turn it to constructive purposes and thus to the aim of global social justice?

Many people hope that global justice will emerge from a world consensus on minimum standards. But how can this consensus be achieved? Do we need a global institution to fulfil these hopes? Hasn't the dream of centralist control just proved elusive? There is, however, something that we can do. We have a good chance of regaining control if we also globalize politics, and by this I mean politics in the broadest sense, including the economic, social, and cultural areas. Globality forces a foreign policy dimension upon all these areas of politics. In order to control globality, instead of being controlled by it, we must activate these foreign policy dimensions.

Classical foreign policy, which for 350 years has been conceived as politics of nation states towards other nation states, must change its self-perception. If it does not wish to become irrelevant, it must adapt to the new world. It needs a conceptual retooling. In order to do justice to the world of the twenty-first century, it must catch up with the process of globalization, it must radically expand and diversify its targets and instruments.

Some had calculated that after the dissolution of the bipolar system the future would belong to the nation states again, with 189 states as independent players in the international system instead of the two superpowers. They were wrong! Whilst it is true that the process of globalization went hand in hand with processes of fragmentation, it was not only the two ideological blocs which became fragmented. Other big collective entities also began to crumble, including the nation state itself. In addition to national governments, countless transnational players in the economy and in society, science and culture, technology, and ecology had long since started to assert their interests and spread their messages at the global level. CNN, the Red Cross, Yehudi Menuhin, political scientists at Harvard University, the Internet, and Greenpeace, not to mention multinational corporations, now bring their influence to bear on foreign policy in a decentralized, autonomous manner. World citizens and global civil societies already exist, even if we do not yet have a World Constitution.

At the same time, the end of the bipolar system opened up new possibilities for action for old and new players above the nation state level. Multilateral initiatives still frequently fail in the UN Security Council, but they no longer automatically fall foul of the self-interested veto of one or other major power. The intervention in Bosnia was based on a mandate from the Security Council. Those in Kosovo and Iraq took place without a mandate, but in accordance with resolutions of the United Nations to prevent genocide and on the nonproliferation of weapons of mass destruction. Those who accuse NATO and the United State of not having a mandate in these cases must at least face up to the question of whether they wish to tolerate genocide or the proliferation of weapons of mass destruction whenever a permanent member of the Security Council sees fit to use its veto for reasons of national interest.

Moreover, a new body of international criminal law is emerging. War criminals and perpetrators of genocide can no longer count on escaping unpunished. The World Trade Organization has been founded, NATO and the EU are enlarging to the East. With the euro, the first supranational monetary union since the end of the gold standard has been formed. People in Asia and America are wondering how the exchange rates of the euro against the dollar and the yen will develop. Who can doubt that all of this is far beyond the horizon of nation states' classical foreign policy?

Then, however, we have to ask: What will be the results of the uncontrolled interaction of the foreign policy interests of subnational, national, and supranational communities? Is "Responsible Globality" not a contradiction in terms? Do we have to reckon with chaos? Or can we rely on all concerned to realize that communication and cooperation are in their own best interest?

A world government may still be a vision of the future. I believe, however, that—even without such a government—international politics has already evolved into a world domestic politics: the sum of the work of the countless bearers of foreign policy messages that I have just described. In nation states, too, at least the democratic ones, politics is by no means a matter for governments alone; rather, it relates to thousands of concerns and interests. The question is simply whether or not we can be satisfied with the results of such a world domestic politics.

And we can only be satisfied if we manage to make the transition from the centuries-old politics of national interest to an era of responsible global politics. At present, I see only a very few who are willing to take on global responsibility. The United States is occasionally accused of taking on the role of world policeman. But let me ask you, what would we do without the United States when the Security Council is paralyzed? We would have to invent it, or rouse ourselves to act. Apart from the United States, I can see almost no one on the world stage willing and able to assume global responsibility. Just think about the necessity of taking the lead in human rights issues, or in seeking peaceful solutions to conflicts, for instance in the Middle East. What would we do without the United States? International politics relies on the American ability and willingness to make decisions, just as the world economy relies on American dynamism. If only more nation states showed such responsibility!

World domestic policies could produce excellent results if as many participants as possible were to follow certain maxims in their foreign policy. For lack of a world government, foreign policy maxims cannot be decreed, but they would reflect an "imperative of responsibility," to use a phrase coined by the philosopher Hans Jonas. It would be in the long-term interest of all concerned for each individual player to follow them on a voluntary basis, and hence participate in a predictable manner in what I would like to call the community of global responsibility. Maxims of decentralized action can lead to concerted strategies of a preventive global foreign policy. By creating an awareness of mutual interests, preventive foreign policy would nip crises in the bud instead of waiting to try to heal them when they have already broken out. It would lead to greater international coordination and to closer webbed global cooperation.

I would like to name eight such maxims, hoping that this Forum will lend its support in disseminating them among all concerned.

First, each foreign policy player should regard it as being his responsibility to promote the global spread of democracy as a strategy for peace. While Kant's thesis that democracies do not go to war against one another may not always hold, it has been impressively confirmed in Europe since 1945, and has assumed central significance since the 1970s in Africa, Asia, and Latin America as well. There can be no lasting peace without democracy, either domestically or with one's international neighbors.

Second, let me make a case for the protection of fundamental human rights as a worldwide minimum standard, since it is the first step on the path towards democracy. We did after all celebrate the fiftieth anniversary of the Universal Declaration of Human Rights in 1998.

Third, we have to renounce nationalism, the arms race, and traditional power politics. All of these arise from nineteenth century-thinking that we have largely left behind us in Europe. A repetition of historical European mistakes in other parts of the globe would spell disaster for the entire world.

My fourth maxim is not to replace the ideological confrontation of the Cold War with scenarios of global cultural wars—as if the human race could not do very well without the law of the jungle. Admittedly, we do observe fundamentalist violence—and attempts are made to justify it on cultural and religious grounds—on a daily basis in all parts of the world. If we take a closer look, however, these alleged clashes of civilizations are not clashes of different cultures, but inevitably uncivilized behavior within cultures. We must prevent these breakdowns of cilivization from becoming global conflicts.

My fifth maxim aims at foregoing "beggar thy neighbor" policies in the globalized economy. Competitive devaluations, social dumping, and protectionism have turned out to be unsuitable attempts to solve one's own problems to the detriment of one's trading partners. We would fall into a downward spiral in the world economy, even a depression comparable only with the world economic crisis of seventy years ago, if such patterns of policy won the day. Thus, going against this maxim would be utterly irrational.

Sixth, we should actively pursue a strategy of communication as a means of confidence building. Europe has used the Organization for Security and Cooperation in Europe (OSCE)—a process of communication beyond ideological and geographical borders—as an effective means of supporting and smoothing the historical breakthrough towards overcoming the bipolar division of Europe and Germany. I am of the opinion that this pattern could be repeated in many places in the world.

As a seventh maxim, I propose global and inter-cultural learning and research in order to solve practical problems. We need a global learning and research community to meet the major challenges of our time, which are global in nature, such as the stabilization of the world economy, the restoration of the ecological equilibrium, or the fight against international crime. This is also true of the tasks of peacekeeping, conflict prevention, and settlement of disputes that concern us all.

Let me just point out two impressive examples of the possibility of learning in economic policy that are certainly inter-cultural. In the 1980s the United States learned very actively from Japanese models of pre-competitive research cooperation in microelectronics, and Japan and Europe have every reason in the 1990s to take a lesson from the American model of combining budgetary discipline, monetary pragmatism, and knowledge-based growth.

With my eighth and final maxim, I would like to call for improved use of existing instruments of international and interregional cooperation—particularly regional integration above nation state level. I am not only thinking of the European Union, which—by introducing the euro—has just taken a decisive step towards integration, a step that will at the same time dramatically change the global monetary system. NAFTA, SADC, ASEAN, Mercosur, and other groupings demonstrate that the idea of regional integration has taken root everywhere.

It is up to us to translate these maxims into concrete strategies for preventive foreign policy. "Good governance" should guide us as our aim and standard in international political action. We should also clarify together what we understand by "good governance" and how we are to measure it. Let us develop a new, clear understanding of the requirements of preventive action, of the means and resources needed for this purpose, and let us try to win domestic support for this endeavor.

This will be simpler in our societies once the fact that everyone is affected by global risks has taken root in the public awareness. In some areas this awareness has already developed. I am thinking of the environment, where conduct in one part of the world has massive consequences in other parts. I am also thinking of transnational crime, which can no longer be effectively contained by national politics. Above all, however, I am thinking of the world economic system, which witnessed a great deal of capital market turbulence last year, a turbulence seen as equally threatening everywhere.

There are other developments that concern us all, the consequences of which we have not yet understood. How, for instance, are we to solve the problems arising from demographic developments—rapid population growth in the developing countries on the one hand and a growing number of pensioners in the mature industrialized nations on the other? How are we to deal with the dissolution of social cohesion and the omnipotence of economic competitiveness at the cost of solidarity?

The first precondition for preventive action is for us to give our societies the freest possible structure. Open, free societies have unique sources of strength. They provide access to all decentralized sources of ideas in the fields of politics, economics, science, and culture. Some may still find this paradoxical, but I believe that European history is the most conspicuous proof that free societies, in spite of all the democratic disputes, all their creative unrest, are more stable and peaceful in the long term than unfree, regulated, and administrated societies. We therefore need to refute policies that thwart reforms because of cowardice, opportunism, or fear of a loss of power. Citizens are perfectly aware that it is they who, in the end, have to pay the price for such failings. We therefore have to put a stop to political paranoia.

We need only think of the crises of the past few years in order to reflect on the advantages of preventive strategies as opposed to subsequent damage control, e.g. the currency and capital market crises in Asia, Russia, and Latin America. There is a need here for "crash-barriers" around the markets to prevent panic reactions and to create confidence in the reliability of the markets. One key to greater stability and predictability would be international coordination of the economic policies among the leading industrialized nations. Such coordination should not be condemned as an unutterable "'C' word," but rather should be used as a pattern of responsibly dealing with globalization. If, as is the case at present, the danger of worldwide deflation cannot be ruled out, it is the responsibility of those governments and central banks that still have scope for action to help stimulate the world economy. This is true even if one's own national economy does not yet appear to have been infected by deflation. In this area as well, preventive action is more efficient than crisis management after the fact.

Recent European and Japanese proposals for stabilizing the exchange rates between the euro, the dollar, and the yen should not be discarded summarily as mere heresy, either. May I recall that coordinated management of exchange rates played a role in the coordinated devaluation of the dollar under the 1985 Plaza Agreement, and again in shoring up the dollar in the summer of 1995. Why should something like this not be possible in the future as well?

The latest crises on the financial markets in South East Asia or in Russia are undoubtedly also due to inadequate banking supervision in these countries. Would it not be possible for, say, the IMF, the World Bank, and the EBRD to jointly develop rules for assessing of solvency and credits risks for banks and to enforce and safeguard these rules internationally through effective controls?

The long-term strategic aim should be worldwide adherence to rules of a social market economy that combines the welfare gains offered by the markets with protection against severe social disruptions. By developing the social market economy after the War, Germany was able to increase the ability of the capitalist system to produce social integration. Some proponents of "laissez-faire" criticize this as heresy. This accusation, however, does not invalidate the idea of a social market economy. To be sure,

Germany does not intend to teach anyone a lesson, and indeed there is no need for this.

After all, Adam Smith himself called for public infrastructures in education and health care and for the protection of workers against social hardship. A frequently overlooked fact is that the great economist was also a moral philosopher for whom the invisible hand of the market was not an end in itself, but a means to eliminate "barbarian circumstances."

If we are to have a satisfactory world domestic politics, it must be founded on a world social order. Performance, efficiency, and social balancing must be integrated the world over if we are to achieve not only social, but also political and economic stability at global level.

Finally, as far as the relationship between the levels of decision-making is concerned, ranging from subnational through national and supranational to multinational, a transculturally convincing ordering principle is readily available: decisions should be made at the level where the best information flows together and where they can be best implemented. Switzerland has been practicing this principle for 700 years, the United States for 200 years, Germany since 1949, and the European Union since 1957. This treasure chest of experience is open to everybody.

I am particularly keen on seeing the dialogue between cultures intensified in order to prevent the much-quoted "clash of civilizations." As was the case with arms control in the time of the ideological confrontation between East and West, the dialogue between the cultures is now taking on a confidence-building and hence peacekeeping role. Globalization, as well as the constant technical breakthroughs and the amplifying role of the media, has led to more rapid and intensive interaction between different cultures than ever before in history. This brings opportunities: The freedom to exchange information enriches cultures, keeping them alive and preventing them from collecting dust as in a museum. Greater opening up to information would also facilitate the spreading of truth.

But make no mistake: Our goal should not be a global mass culture. Globalization also provokes contradictions, not so much between the major world cultures as between the forces of modernism and the forces of tradition within cultures. Our world without borders does not always lead to useful integration, but can also lead to a painful loss of identity and sense of belonging. As human beings, we need to feel securely rooted in history and culture. Resentment and stubbornness, on the other hand, can result in intolerance and rejection.

This is why inter-cultural dialogue is so important. Politicians must lead and promote this process. If they fail to do so, the danger arises that conflict-minded sections of society might manipulate tradition, culture, and religion in order to use them as tools in the interest of power politics or economic competition. This we must prevent. Our thinking in this field should extend beyond material things. Aung San Suu Kyi, the champion of democracy and human rights in Myanmar, considers that some of the less palatable aspects of Western societies are due not to democracy, but to modern materialism which ignores cultural and human values, and where money reigns supreme. She is quite right. We must not forget the human soul.

I also feel highly encouraged by the Iranian President Mohammad Khatami. He has called on the Islamic societies not to hide inside the fortress of tradition, but to open up to the modern world, without falling prey to unbridled materialism. His call for a dialogue between the religions and his initiative for an "International Year of Cultural Dialogue" deserve every support. They appear to me to herald a policy of building confidence through greater knowledge of and greater respect for one another.

So you can see that what I am advocating is no less than a fundamental change in our thinking. Globalization in thinking must replace the intellectual status quo. The human being must be made the focus of all political activity. Only then can we see globalization not as a threat, but as a challenge with a high potential for a new quality of cooperation, aimed at giving a positive shape to the twenty-first century. It would be wrong to close our eyes to globalization.

Secretary General Kofi Annan envisages a dialogue of a worldwide civil society for the next millennium. The United Nations therefore sees the world community as a worldwide community of responsibility. Let us even go one step further and see the world community as a community of opportunity! Let us leave behind the anarchy of nation-state politics. Let us use the interplay of globalized foreign policies as world domestic policy. The international system of nation states can thus develop into a global political system. Let us pin our hopes even today on the citizens of this world community. In this way, the century of war can be followed by a century of peace.

We all know that so far this is only an opportunity. Nevertheless, it is an opportunity of which we should never again lose sight.

PART II

Comments

CHAPTER 8

Cross-Cultural Judgments[1]

Amitai Etzioni

THE DEBATE between those who argue that we should not pass judgment on the conduct of other people and those who champion universal human rights or other global values is making significant progress. It has achieved several points of broadly based, albeit not unanimous, cross-cultural consensus. Reviewing these points of near-agreement may enable future deliberations to treat these points as their base line, seeking convergence on issues about which the various sides are still far apart.

Thinkers increasingly agree that relativism is a position that has played an important historical role but is difficult now to sustain. Historically there was good reason to be troubled by the tendency of Western people to view other societies as "primitive," "barbarian," or inferior and to seek to impose their values on other cultures and people. Much of anthropology has, in effect, been dedicated to challenging this Western view and helping members of Western societies understand and appreciate other cultures. While the need for such didactic work is far from obviated, the danger of a strong bias in the opposite direction has come into evidence during the last decades. I refer to the great reluctance of Western intellectuals to pass judgment on behavior in other cultures such as genital mutilation, child labor, detention without trial, caning, and amputating the limbs of thieves. While such refusals to lay moral claims take many forms, and are deeply anchored in classical liberalism, the form most relevant to the discussion of international relations is cultural relativism, according to which each community should set its own values and needs not make any account to others about the legitimacy of such choices.

If one considers the early Western sense of general superiority (as distinct from having merit in some areas but not in others) as a "thesis," and the rise of cross-cultural relativism as the "antithesis," we seem to be moving into a period of synthesis. There is growing agreement, even in non-Western countries, that some forms of cross-cultural judgments are appropriate. For instance, Bilahari Kausikan of Singapore (whose intellectuals have been strong players in this debate[2]), flatly states, "Human rights have become a legitimate issue in interstate relations. How a country treats its citizens is no longer a matter for its own exclusive determination."[3] He even recognizes, "Others can and do legitimately claim a concern."[4] Onuma Yasuaki, Japan's leading human rights expert, reports that there is increasing recognition that "states can no longer conveniently deny the universality of human rights. Nor can they claim that human rights are exclusively domestic questions. . . . [T]he seemingly irreconcilable conflict between universalists and relativists is more theoretical than real. There is actually a wide range of consensus that most of the alleged human rights must be universally protected."[5] Indeed, as President Herzog has put it, such a "search for consensus . . . is not something we should give up lightly."

Consensus on the need to protect the environment is a strong example of growing international consensus[6]—allowing of course for great differences in emphasis and willingness to implement policies.

I am not suggesting that the controversy between relativists and universalists is dying or that all agree to some universal notion of the need to respect human dignity (the term "rights" is often avoided by non-Westerners) but only that there is now a mainstream agreement, and those who do not participate in it rapidly are becoming outliers.[7]

Second, there is a growing recognition that the flow of *moral claims does not run only in one direction.* While the West is gaining a following in other countries for its political freedom concerns, Asian claims that it has allowed the deterioration of social harmony and moral virtues are not falling on deaf ears. And the claims of many non-Westerners that socioeconomic rights also are important are supported by quite a few Western intellectuals and ideologues for various reasons. (Socioeconomic rights also are included in the German constitution.)

Third, there is a school of thought that argues that the moral claims one society lays on another often can be *justified in the other society's tradition,* albeit drawing on different conceptions and narratives. For instance, Daniel A. Bell argues that Islam does not allow *hudud*—the amputation of a thief's hand—under most circumstances. Hence members of non-Islamic cultures can speak up against it by drawing on intra-Islamic rationales rather than on Westerners' conceptions of human rights;[8] this is why studies such as the recent German Trade Book Association's Peace Prize–winner Annemarie Schimmel's work on Islam are so crucial. In the same vein, outsiders to Chinese culture may suggest that the Chinese may come to freedom of inquiry and press because they serve the community rather than because they see them as rights in their own right.[9] And Westerners have many sources in their own cultures that lead them to be concerned about socioeconomic rights. There is no reason, on the other side of the cultural divide, to object to such intra-cultural accounting of moral claims, so long as they are far-reaching and well-grounded. (For instance, subscribing to human rights because they are "useful" for community purposes may provide sound but insufficient grounding.)

Fourth, there is some consensus that different societies need not adopt exactly the same regime to be democratic. Thus, just as there are differences among various Western societies (for instance the United States and the United Kingdom: the latter has no equivalent to the First Amendment freedom of speech and religion, but has a state secret act, and a prohibition on hate speech) so there may be differences among various non-Western societies that are achieving democratic status—say between India and the Philippines.

Finally, there is a growing agreement that there is *a connection between socioeconomic and political development.* At least it is agreed that countries with very low per capita GNP, poor public health, and a very low education level, will tend to have much greater difficulties in introducing democratic regimes than more fully developed countries.[10] Where may the debate move from here?

NEXT STEPS

The End of Economic Deferral

The argument that underdeveloped countries must defer the introduction of human rights and democratic regimes until they are economically developed, or that saving people from starvation and disease must take priority over political development, must be put to rest because it does not withstand elementary empirical observations and moral criticism. While socioeconomic difficulties can hinder political development, these do not make them of less ethical standing than economic achievements. Note that countries such as China and Singapore are deferring not only so-called "soft" democratic rights such as the right of free expression and assembly, but also protection against detention without trial, curbs on press freedoms, seizures of property,[11] and other elementary human rights. Is it better to be tortured and hanged than to face food shortages and possibly even plagues?

The choice posited is a false one, presented in stark terms that favor socioeconomic over political development. The fact is that Singapore already has achieved a very high standard of living—a per capita annual income of $12,000 in 1990, the same level that the United States reached only ten years before[12]—and yet still feels that it is not sufficiently developed to make room for political freedoms. While there are occasional pockets of food shortages in some parts of China, millions of Chinese now are encouraged to pursue optional consumer goods such as gourmet coffee, designer blue jeans, and name-brand makeup and perfumes. These hardly have a higher moral standing than elementary freedoms.

The argument that economic development will not be possible unless political development is deferred is belied both by the experience of India and of course by the history of the West, in which political and economic development took place simultaneously. Indeed, the opposite may be more accurate—that economic development follows political freedoms and not vice versa. Aryeh Neier notes, "Open societies around the world are flourishing economically to a far greater extent than closed societies or societies that were closed until recently."[13]

Notions that political development "must" or "should" (on moral grounds) be deferred until economic development is advanced or achieved should be laid to rest.

The "Need" to Maintain Social Order

Asian political leaders and intellectuals have looked with condescension at the deterioration of the social order in the West and argued that restrictions of political freedoms are needed to sustain social harmony. In a public address, Singapore's Prime Minister, Goh Chok Tong, said,

> Western liberals, foreign media, and human rights groups want Singapore to be like their societies, and some Singaporeans mindlessly dance to their tune. . . . We must think for ourselves and decide what is good for Singapore, what will make Singapore stable and successful. Above all else, stay away from policies which have brought a plague of social and economic problems to the United States and Britain.[14]

Kevin Y.L. Tan, senior lecturer at the National University of Singapore, echoes the prime minister when he writes, "The problem as Asians see it is this: How can the West—especially America—preach democracy and human rights as fundamental values when the West can't even get its own house in order?"[15]

It should be noted first of all that this argument does not comport with the previous, economic one. The economic perspective argues for delaying political freedoms; the social argument suggests that they are inherently incompatible with an orderly and virtuous society.

These arguments are not sustainable. First, the deterioration of social order in the West has been a recent development. The American society of the 1950s, for instance, is held up as a model of social order. While it was less democratic than contemporary America (especially in its treatment of minorities and women), it maintained extensive human rights and political freedoms. Other societies in Western Europe had a high level of social order in the 1960s and beyond.

Second, the Asian societies that rely heavily on the state to maintain order act in a rather different way than they imply when they refer to themselves as "communitarian."[16] In contrast, Japan, which is much more democratic, has a strong social order that is based more on family and community, national bonds and loyalties than on state coercion, comes much closer to a model of a society whose members truly are involved and committed to social harmony and moral values. Coercion is only necessary when people do not voluntarily do what is expected of them. The much lower level of policing in Japan compared to Singapore, without a loss in social order, highlights the difference.

Third, it should be noted that even Japan may put too much weight on social conformity and loyalties. A true communitarian society combines the quest for social order, based largely on the voluntary commitment of its members, with socially constructed opportunities for individual and subgroup expressions and with secure political freedoms. Aside from being right in their own right, such social formations serve to enhance creativity and innovation and to satisfy deep-seated human needs.

And yet the Asians make a major valid point, which if restated highlights a Western failing. Given the communitarian ideal of balance between social order and individual and subgroup autonomy, the West, especially American society, has veered off in the opposite direction. We have allowed self-interest, self-indulgence, permissiveness, and a sense of entitlement to grow excessively while neglecting the foundations of social and moral order. Hence, a strong case can be made that both kinds of societies are converging on a societal model that combines a higher level of social order than the West has recently experienced with a higher level of individual and subgroup autonomy than even Japan currently allows.

Note that in this context it is not helpful to refer to a convergence of East and West, as one may do as a very rough first approximation. Neither "East" nor "West" is of one kind, certainly from the viewpoint of the issues addressed here. The levels of policing, social order, and political development of India and Singapore, Japan and China, the Philippines and Burma hardly are the same. And the state of the American society and that of Scandinavia are rather different. Moreover, few would wish to combine the social order deficiencies of several Western societies with the lack of protection of women's rights, treatment of minorities, and excessive pressure to conform of several Eastern societies. The cross-cultural dialogue will be best served when the discussion focuses on those virtues and social formations that are legitimate and worth extolling and advancing.

Human Rights: Not an Instrument of Western Oppression

One of the most repeated refrains of critics of human rights and democratic regimes is that human rights are Western ideas, that they have been used as legitimation for Western interventions in the lives of other societies. Political theorists Adamantia Pollis and Peter Schwab famously refer to human rights as "a Western construct with limited applicability," arguing that "human rights as a twentieth-century concept and as embedded in the United Nations can be traced to the particular experiences of England, France, and the United States."[17] Marnia Lazreg further claims that "the current U.S.-sponsored drive for human rights necessarily reveals itself as a moralistic ideology that satisfies extramoral needs."[18] These arguments must be unpacked and dealt with separately. They mix points that hinder the needed cross-cultural dialogues with those that contribute to the suggested convergence between East and West.

The argument that human rights are Western in origin and hence not suitable to other cultures is a particularly unfortunate one. Virtues either should be considered valid or rejected; the source of an ideal and its legitimacy should not be confused.

Westerners should not and do not reject "Asian" notions of the beauty and peace that harmony entails; and human rights should not be rejected by other cultures if they are justifiable, even if they were first formulated in the West. The point can be tested by the following mental experiment. Assume for a moment that recent claims by some African American historians that Western notions of political freedom and democracy actually originated in Africa, in Egypt especially, turn out to be valid. Would that enhance the legitimacy of the democratic ideals? And, if yes, only for Africans? Only for North Africans? Clearly, historical accounting has very little to do with the legitimacy of a given virtue.

The second, and more powerful, version of the argument contends that some Western countries have used others' lack of human rights to legitimate their intervention in countries. These interventions range from colonization to the recent landing of Marines in Haiti and economic sanctions imposed on Cuba. A considerable literature on the subject asks under what conditions such interventions are justified (against a new Hitler?), and when are they inappropriate (to advance American corporate interests?).[19] One need not address these questions here, however, because they do not deal with the legitimacy of the claim of human rights any more than they deal with the virtue of social order. They concern the means and conditions under which stronger powers may interfere in the affairs of weaker powers. To push the point, one can be radically opposed to any and all economic sanctions, not to mention blockades and invasions, against countries that violate human rights or are disorderly, and still hold liberty and social rules as core virtues.

In short, one needs to separate the legitimacy of certain moral claims across cultures from the ways and means by which they may be advanced. If a society considers it illegitimate to underwrite its moral claims by use of force or economic means, what force do they have? The answer is the force of moral claims.

The Cross-Societal Moral Voice

As the notions of moral voice and moral dialogues are central to my argument but not widely recognized, they deserve additional elaboration here. The *moral voice* is a peculiar form of motivation that encourages people to adhere to values to which they already subscribe. The term moral voice is particularly appropriate because people "hear" it. Thus, when a person who affirms a value is tempted to ignore it, he or she hears a voice urging him or her to do what is right. Hearing the voice does not mean that one will always or even regularly heed it, but it will often affect behavior. For example, a person who at first ignores the voice may later repent and engage in compensatory behavior. As with individuals, communities too may hear their own moral voices.[20]

Moral dialogues occur when a group of people engages in a process of sorting the values that will guide their lives. Should the sanctity of the unborn child or women's right to choose guide our abortion policy? Should the virtue of a color-blind (nondiscriminating) society or that of reverse discrimination (to correct for past and current injustices) guide our employment policies? Built into this concept are tenets that—to put it carefully—not all members of the society share. These tenets should hence be stated explicitly. Moral dialogues assume that societies need shared formulations of the good and cannot function only on the basis of negotiated settlements between individual and subgroup formations of the good. Moreover, moral dialogues require that the processes that lead to such shared formulations entail dialogues that concern values and not merely deliberations over empirical facts or logically derived notions.[21] Moral dialogues are not merely a matter of reasonable people coming to terms, but of people of divergent convictions finding a common normative ground.[22]

It is relatively easy to demonstrate that such dialogues take place constantly in well-formed societies, which most democracies are, and that frequently they result (albeit sometimes only after prolonged dialogues) in a new affirmed direction for the respective societies. But can moral dialogues take place internationally? and to what effect?

Moral dialogues occurring across national lines are much more limited in scope, intensity, conclusion, and effect than intranational ones. Nevertheless they point to the processes that, if further advanced, can provide a thicker global moral base than the one to which minimalists point. For example, there is a worldwide dialogue about the extent to which "we" (that is, all nations, and in this sense the people of the world) ought to respect the environment. Of course, the dialogue is affected by numerous nonnormative considerations, often dressed up in normative claims. Nonetheless, the dialogue affects what people consider morally appropriate. Thus, one reason most countries try to at least visibly adhere to environmental guidelines is that they do not wish to be seen as acting illegitimately in the eyes of other nations. Among the examples frequently given of rising worldwide consensus on specific environmental matters, reflecting the general rising shared commitment to the protection of the environment, are limitations on whaling, on trade in African elephant ivory, on trade in hazardous waste, and on adding to acid rain and ozone layer damage, among others.[23]

Moral voices are applied *to* superpowers and not merely *by* them to less powerful countries. (Indeed, some have argued that relying on moral claims is the special province of less powerful nations.[24] A case in point was the worldwide condemnation of the United States following the 1992 Earth Summit in Rio de Janeiro where the United States forced a watering-down of the climate control treaty and refused to sign the biodiversity treaty. These acts drew heavy criticism from all over the world.)

A Communitarian Call for Cross-Cultural Moral Dialogues

To help nourish cross-national moral dialogues, communitarians should favor a step opposite that taken by cultural relativists. Namely, the cross-cultural expression of moral voices that truly reflect the people of a society.

It is necessary to raise moral voices across societal lines, to seek to identify and articulate a core of globally shared values. The need for, and legitimacy of, laying moral claims on societies other than one's own, appreciating the drives of other societies when they advance individual rights and shoulder social responsibilities, and censoring them when they do not, must be recognized, I deliberately refer to *laying moral claims.* It is a rather different matter than when a nation attempts to impose values by sending in the Marines, Special Forces, or the Foreign Legion, by erecting blockades, or otherwise applying military or economic force to promote its values. Such coercive measures do not build a moral community and are justified only under extreme conditions (the next Nazi regime) discussed in the literature on just wars. While only powerful nations can employ military or economic power to push values, even the smallest of nations can exercise the moral voice, as demonstrated at various points by Costa Rica, Mexico, the Scandinavian countries, Switzerland, and Israel.

To call on all people to respect the same set of core values does not entail arguing that all have to follow the same path of economic development, enjoy the same music, or exercise the same table manners. At issue are core values such as respecting human dignity by not warring or tolerating genocide, government responsiveness to all the members of a nation's respective communities and not only small elites,[25] and the upholding of select values rather than the pursuit of pervasive agendas. Indeed, it is a sociological mistake, when international bodies do meet to discuss normative issues, for each of the participants to add all that is on their normative wish list to the pile of cross-national moral claims. The long road to a world of shared values will be shortened somewhat if the focus is kept on a limited set of core values.

The cross-cultural moral voice cannot avoid addressing the political development of countries that do not respect autonomy or that attempt to coerce order rather than foment it on moral grounds. True, just as there are differences among communitarian societies, so there may be different pathways to a democratic polity. Because of the close connection between the democratic form of government and communitarian core virtues, however, fostering democratic forms of government (broadly conceived, not merely comprising regular voting) is a pivotal and necessary part of a cross-national moral dialogue. As President Herzog has declared regarding fundamentalist authoritarian states,

> Those who speak of "fundamentalism" today usually, and not always without reason, associate it with the humiliation of women, inhumane punishment for thieves and adulteresses, and attacks on writers and journalists who have fallen into disfavor. In reality, what we commonly describe as fundamentalism is nothing but an instrumentalization of religious sentiments for political purposes, a blatant bid for totalitarian power. The threat of this abuse of religion is particularly prevalent where social hardship and a lack of established rights offer a breeding-ground for manipulation of the masses. . . . [T]hese are phenomena which we cannot accept under any circumstances nor tolerate for foreign-policy reasons or on the grounds of a weakly ethical relativism. When we enter into a dialogue with others we bring in some basic precepts which are not negotiable.[26]

Rather than muting the cross-cultural moral voice, as the cultural relativists do, all societies should respect the right of others to lay moral claims on them just as they are entitled to do the same.

Thus, the West should realize that it is well within its legitimate, world community-building role when it criticizes China for its violation of human rights. And China should be viewed as equally legitimate when it criticizes American society for its neglect of filial duties. To reiterate, as long as moral claims are laid as moral claims, rather than as justification for coercive measures, they help lay the groundwork for needed moral dialogues.

To form cross-cultural judgments requires another layer of accountability: substantive global values, in the sense that they lay a claim on all and are not particular to any one community or society. Thus, as I see it, individual rights do not reflect a Western value (even if historically they arose in the West), but a global value that lays claims on all people. Far from being deterred or chastened when the Chinese government, or some Asian intellectuals, protest the West's application of the value of individual rights to Asian cultures and regimes, I see in the furor that such claims generate a recognition of the validity of these claims. And for that same reason, I find Asian intellectual's call on the West—for example, to enhance our respect of the elderly—also fully legitimate and compelling.

Cross-cultural moral claims are effective *because* they resonate with values we share, but have neglected. This is a major reason Asians become distressed when they are criticized for not sufficiently respecting individual rights. If one instead chastised them for using chopsticks instead of forks, they would hardly be perturbed. Similarly, Asians make telling points when they criticize the West about its neglect of social order. Compare the effect of such claims to those of a call by Muslims on the West to embrace Islamic divorce laws. Nobody would respond in a guilty furor; rather, people would ignore such normative appeals or laugh them out of court. Not all cross-cultural moral claims are heard, though it is rather evident which are. And, as President Herzog states, fear of negative reactions to such moral criticisms should not deter the international community from making them: "it is . . . wrong to think that the only choice available is between silence in the face of human rights abuses in other countries and an infringement upon those countries' sovereignty."[27]

I should add in this context that President Herzog recognizes the commonalities between the Asian East and the West as well as between Islam and the West. One may wonder if his generosity of spirit carries him just a bit too far in his discussion of the similarities of Germany and Japan. Japan still has considerable ground to cover in its recognition of gender equality and minority rights (for instance for Koreans), in its treatment of handicapped persons, and in coming to terms with its past.

All this is not to deny that there are signs that the international moral voice does not fall on completely deaf ears. For example, it is reported that, after having ignored human rights issues for years, in Asian countries "human rights [are] no longer dismissed as a tool of foreign oppression but [are] promoted as a means of asserting Asian distinctiveness."[28] China seems to have reformed some of its most grievous orphanages and labor camps under pressure from Amnesty International and other moral voices.[29] Even in countries such as Cambodia and Myanmar, one now hears voices that come from within—and not from Western critics—opposing authoritarian rule in the name of human rights and democracy. Thus an opposition leader recently argued in Cambodia that "no human being should be asked to choose between bread and freedom."[30]

Recognizing the need to raise moral voices globally does not legitimize berating other people cross-culturally, any more than it legitimizes berating other members of one's own community. The moral voice is most compelling when it is firm but not screeching; judging but not judgmental; critical but not self-righteous.

We can acknowledge quite readily that those who champion global values themselves do not always heed their call; but this observation does not invalidate the standing of those values. And one might recognize that a society chastised for failing to adhere to one universal value may even provide a shining example for the rest of the world to follow in terms of a different universal value. But none of these observations argues that bringing strong substantive values to the nascent worldwide dialogue is to be denied; on the contrary, it is a reflection of commitment to these values. At the same time, one must take into account that until the world dialogue of convictions is much more advanced, and a much stronger worldwide core of values has evolved, worldwide shared values cannot serve as a satisfactory frame for societal values. Even if a truly democratic global parliament, after properly constructed worldwide megalogues, could formulate public policies, or moral assessments, wouldn't they still need to be judged by some other moral criteria? The crowning test may well need to be found elsewhere.

NOTES

1. An earlier version of this essay was published in the *Journal of Social Philosophy* 28, no. 3 (Winter 1997). Reprinted by permission of the *Journal of Social Philosophy.*
2. See for example the work of Singaporean diplomat Kishore Mahbubani, "Asia's Cultural Fusion," *Foreign Affairs* 74, no.1 (January/February 1995), 100-110, and "The Dangers of Decadence: What the Rest Can Teach the West," *Foreign Affairs* 72, no. 4 (September/October 1993), 10-14. See also the remarks of Singapore's former Prime Minister Lee Kuan Yew, reported by Erik Kuhonta, "On Social and Economic Rights," *Human Rights Dialogue* 2, (September 1995), 3. For a detailed review of exchanges between Singaporeans and Americans, see Donald K. Emmerson, "Singapore and the 'Asian Values' Debate," *Journal of Democracy* 6, no. 4 (October 1995), 95-104.
3. Bilahari Kausikan, "Asia's Different Standard," *Foreign Policy* Vol. 92 (Fall 1993), 24.
4. Ibid.
5. Yasuaki Onuma, "In Quest of Intercivilizational Human Rights: 'Universal' vs. 'Relative' Human Rights Viewed from an Asian Perspective." Center for Asian Pacific Affairs, The Asia Foundation, Occasional Paper No. 2 (March 1996), 8.
6. See Amitai Etzioni, *The New Golden Rule: Community and Morality in a Democratic Society* (New York: Basic Books, 1997), 230-231.
7. Aryeh Neier, *The Responsive Community* 7, no. 3 (Summer 1997), 25-26.

8. Daniel A. Bell, "The East Asian Challenge to Human Rights: Reflections on an East West Dialogue," *Human Rights Quarterly* 18 (Johns Hopkins University Press: August 1996), 664.
9. Ibid., 658.
10. Seymor Martin Lipset, et al. "A comparative analysis of the social requisites of democracy," *Comparative Political Sociology*, no. 136, May 1993, 155-156.
11. Kausikan openly states as much. Op cit., 38.
12. Compare numbers in George Thomas Kurian, *Datapoedia of the United States 1790-2000* (Bernan Press, 1994), 90; and *The 1993 Britannica Book of the Year* (Encyclopedia Britannica, 1993), 796.
13. Aryeh Neier, "Asia's Unacceptable Standard," *Foreign Policy*, Vol. 92 (Fall 1993), 42-43.
14. Goh Chok Tong, "Social Values, Singapore Style," *Current History* Vol. 93, no. 9 (December 1994), 422.
15. Kevin Y.L. Tan, Senior Lecturer, Faculty of Law, National University of Singapore, "What Asians Think about the West's Response to the Human Rights Debate," *Human Rights Dialogue* 4 (March 1996), 4.
16. Bilhari Kausikan, "Asian Versus 'Universal' Human Rights," *The Responsive Community* 7, no.3 (Summer 1997).
17. Adamantia Pollis and Peter Schwab, eds. *Human Rights: Cultural and Ideological Perspectives* (New York: Praeger Publishers, 1979), 1, 4.
18. Marnia Lazreg, "Human Rights, State and Ideology: An Historical Perspective," ibid, 41.
19. See, for example, Michael Walzer, *Just and Unjust Wars: A Moral Argument with Historical Illustrations* (New York: Basic Books, 1977).
20. For more discussion, see Etzioni, op cit., "The Moral Voice," 119-126.
21. For a justification of this point, see Etzioni, op cit., 102-104, 227-31.
22. Cf., Amy Gutmann, "The Challenge of Multiculturalism in Political Ethics," *Philosophy and Public Affairs* 22 (Summer 1993), 197ff.
23. Gareth Porter and Janet Welsh Brown, *Global Environmental Politics* (Westview Press: 1996), 69-105.
24. See Minivera Etzioni, *The Majority of One: Towards a Theory of Regional Compatibility* (Beverly Hills, CA: Sage Publications, 1970).
25. See Etzioni, "The Responsive Community: A Communitarian Perspective," *American Sociological Review* 61 (February 1996), 1-11; and *The Active Society: A Theory of Societal and Political Processes* (New York: Free Press, 1968), part four.
26. Speech by Herr Roman Herzog, President of the Federal Republic of Germany, on the occasion of the Award of the 1995 Peace Prize of the German Book Trade Association to Frau Annemarie Schimmel, Frankfurt, 15 October 1995.
27. Federal President Roman Herzog on the Rights of Human Beings. An Essay.
28. Joanne Bauer, "International Human Rights and Asian Commitment," *Human Rights Dialogue* Vol. 3 (December 1995), 1.
29. Amnesty International, "China: Law Reform and Human Rights—Not Far Enough," Feb. 28, 1997. Available at http://www.oil.ca/amnesty/news/1997/31701597.htm.
30. Cited in "Asia: Who Speaks for the People?" *The Economist* Vol. 338 (January 27, 1996), 31.

CHAPTER 9

Inter-Cultural Dialogue versus Confrontation

Hans Küng

THERE WERE INDICATIONS of it at the end of the First World War in 1918; it emerged after the Second World War in 1945; and it became obvious after the collapse of the Soviet system in 1989: humankind has left behind the modern Eurocentric paradigm established at the beginning of the modern European era and entered into a new polycentric constellation, a truly global paradigm.

But many statesmen, not only in Europe, still think and act in terms of outdated "Realpolitik," which is clearly oriented to national or regional power interests. The new paradigm would not merely represent an "idealistic politics" inspired solely by moral principles. Such moralism would face inevitable failure given the reality of power interests. The new paradigm requires statesmen to practice a politics of responsibility that—and this is the art of postmodern statesmanship—at once tries to take seriously ideals and realities, principles and interests, rights and obligations. The global society urgently requires a dialogue of the cultures and is slowly, ever so slowly, developing a minimum of common moral values, standards, and attitudes, a "global ethic," accepted by the various religions, believers and non-believers.

I know of no active statesman who is as unambiguously and energetically committed to this program as the seventh President of the Federal Republic of Germany, Professor Roman Herzog. He quite simply has the necessary credibility that derives from his keen intellect and knowledge, his moral integrity and rectitude, his unforced humanity and sociableness. Knowing President Roman Herzog not only through his speeches and articles, but having accompanied him on state visits to Malaysia, Israel, and Jordan and having had the opportunity to observe him without bias (not only thanks to my Swiss passport), I can confirm the value of such basic attitudes and politics. In his encounters with non-Europeans from many different cultures, Roman Herzog is, in a manner of speaking, living proof that a "clash of civilizations" can be avoided and overcome. Statesmen like him deserve the support not only of politicians but also of academics, intellectuals and journalists. I am delighted to make a contribution to this endeavor. Since President Herzog's commitment to a "dialogue of cultures" is an antithesis to Samuel Huntington's thesis of a "clash of civilizations"—although it is in fact much more than this—I will start my own consideration of this thesis with a personal reminiscence.

I. WHERE HUNTINGTON IS RIGHT

It was back in the early 1980s that I first had the ideas I put into words in 1984: "No world peace without religious peace."[1] In

1989 I submitted this program to discussion at a UNESCO colloquium in Paris[2] and also to the World Economic Forum in Davos, and in 1990 I developed it further within the broad framework of my book *Global Responsibility: In Search of a New World Ethic.*[3] The initial basic premise "no peace amongst the nations without peace amongst the religions" had given birth to a second: "no survival of our world without a global ethic."

Our need for a global ethic was the theme of a lecture I gave in the Dag Hammarskjöld Library Auditorium at UN Headquarters in New York in 1992. I expounded the subject further in the same venue in 1994 and discussed the newly published essay by the Director of the Institute of Strategic Studies at Harvard University, Samuel P. Huntington, that had attracted such attention, "The Clash of Civilizations?"[4]

As a theologian who had for so long endeavored to ensure that the reality of the role of religions for global policy and global peace is taken seriously, I was very gratified to note that Huntington, a prominent political scientist—and even better, one from the Realist school—unlike superficial politicians and political scientists, had at last come out and acknowledged the conscious/subconscious depths of global political conflicts and had thus drawn attention to the fundamental role of the religions in global politics. Quite unlike Huntington's Harvard colleague Henry Kissinger, who, in his monumental work *Diplomacy,* did not find the subject worthy of the slightest mention. Huntington's starting point, after all, fitted badly into Kissinger's scheme of traditional politics of interest; the fact that people can have fundamental religious interests that can certainly influence world policy had obviously never occurred to Kissinger.[5] Since the appearance of Huntington's article, however, more and more political scientists have noticed that the multipolarity of global policy also encompassed multipolarity of religions and multipolarity of cultures.

For an assessment of future conflict potentials it is undoubtedly important to take seriously the idea that the conflicts of world politics may be played out precisely between groups and nations from different cultures. Food for thought: the national borders drawn in Eastern Europe and Africa by the Realist politicians of the modern age are fading before the age-old borders established in the past by tribes, religions, and faiths. Lines of conflict have emerged between Armenia and Azerbaijan, between Georgia and Russia, between Ukraine and Russia, between the different ethnic groups in Yugoslavia in particular, and finally between the Hutu and Tutsi in various states in Central Africa.

So Huntington is not wrong in his forecast that realistically one must expect culturally generated conflicts in the future. And not only for "geopolitical" reasons: because the world is growing ever smaller, the interactions between people of different cultures are expanding and the significance of the real economic blocs increasing. But also for cultural and religious reasons: differences between the cultures are real, often ancient, and range from child-rearing methods to the concept of the state and the understanding of God and nature. And it is precisely where people are disappointed and disadvantaged by the socioeconomic process of modernization and globalization that they are increasingly returning to their own religious roots, which are less changeable and dispensable than political and economic ones.

So Huntington is right in all this, but nevertheless I do not feel able to agree with him in his basic precepts, for the following reasons.

II. WHERE HUNTINGTON IS WRONG

In the discussion following my New York lecture in 1994, some American participants expressed the suspicion that Huntington, who had for many years been an adviser to the Pentagon, was merely looking for a new theory to justify additional expenditure on armaments. I cannot pass judgement. However, Huntington went on to expand his essay, whose title still bore a question mark, into a book, which bears no question mark.[6] He is now propagating his allegedly proven theory as nothing short of a new paradigm of foreign policy, to replace the First-Second-Third World paradigm.

My objections relate primarily to Huntington's theory of cultural circles, which, following on from Arnold Toynbee, he intensifies as the "clash of civilizations." I would like to counter this with three points:

1. Huntington's clash theory feigns a simple system of coordinates: without looking too closely, Huntington determines major civilizations in terms of religion: the Islamic, Hindu, Confucian, Slavic-Orthodox civilizations. But in other cases this is precisely what he does not do: he speaks of Western civilization and Japanese civilization. In doing so, he overlooks the fact that the contrasts within, for instance, Islam are often greater than are those between Islam and the West. The most recent wars have very often been fought between rivals from the same civilization: Iran and Iraq, Iraq and Kuwait, in Somalia, in Rwanda . . . And why do Australia and Israel belong to the West, while Latin America and Eastern Europe do not?
2. Huntington's clash theory promotes bloc-based thinking: he demarcates the seven or eight "civilizations" as if they were monoliths. As if they did not in reality overlap and frequently interpenetrate—even in the big European and American cities.
3. Huntington's clash theory ignores what civilizations have in common: within a single Christendom he separates the Eastern Orthodox from the Western or the Western North American from the Latin American civilization and constantly focuses on the differences between these cultures,

> without taking any note at all of fundamental similarities—not to mention things they have in common with Islam and Judaism.

And this brings me to my decisive objection: a clash of cultures and religions is not inevitable! Not only do I feel unable to accept Huntington's cultural circle theory as "the best compass for the future." I cannot share his fatalism either: his map of the world seems to me to be much too simple. His interest in the continued dominance of the "Euro-American West," which cannot be allowed to become multicultural (a multicultural America is an impossibility, he says, because a non-Western America is not American), is all too transparent. He is very obviously keen to "maintain Western technological and military superiority over other civilizations"[7]: "in the clash of civilizations Europe and America will hang together, or hang separately."[8] In this way, of course, further self-authorized military interventions by the United States and the United Kingdom without a UN mandate can be easily justified.

In the last chapter of his book Huntington provides the military and representatives of the arms industry with brilliant arguments, describing in great detail the horrific scenario of a global war waged by the United States, Europe, Russia, and India against China and most of Islam. Thus he presents the new "natural" enemies of the West following the collapse of communism: Islam and China (all we need is those Islamic terrorists who allegedly threaten the entire world). With a prognosis like this, it is easy for the United States to forego the "peace dividend" in favor of a new, expensive arms euphoria.

To my mind there is a fundamental doubt about whether, after the Cold War and the system of bipolar fronts, a uniform global explanatory model actually exists at all in today's multipolar world. Instead of being captivated by the "clash of civilizations" scenario, we should proceed to a sober assessment of the global situation. We should take the cultural-religious dimension of world politics seriously but without imposing it on all other dimensions. Perhaps a consensus in this spirit could be arrived at in the current discussion. I would formulate it as follows.

III. WHAT CAN BE AGREED UPON

1. One must concede this much to the Realists of world politics: the vast majority of foreign-policy conflicts, even in this postmodern era, are about territory, raw materials, trade, and money. In other words, they revolve around economic, political, and military power interests.
2. In turn, the Realists must concede this: ethnic and religious differences and rivalries may not be the all-explaining paradigm or system of coordinates for all territorial confrontations, economic rivalries, and power interests, but they do constitute the permanent underlying structures by which political, economic, and military conflicts have from time immemorial been justified, inspired, and dramatized, as well as defused and settled.
3. The cultures or—less ambiguously—the religions thus do not constitute the easily mapped surface dimension of all conflicts, but with their utterly different paradigms they do provide the depth—which on no account must be neglected—of many antagonisms and conflicts between the nations, and often even more so within nations, in individual towns, schools, indeed even families.
4. Conclusion: The allegedly inevitable global clash of cultures can at best serve as a new wellspring of fear as required by certain military strategists. But the forward-looking vision for humanity is different: global peace between the religions and cultures, into which we must put all our energy and

which is a prerequisite and engine for global peace between the nations.

Could Huntington agree with this program? Only in the last five pages of his book does he mention what he has sorely neglected over the previous five hundred pages and what, with hindsight, sets his whole book in context: the fact that "the world's major religions . . . also share key values in common," so that a "principle of commonalities" must be formulated for peace in a multicultural world; "peoples in all civilizations should search for and attempt to expound values, institutions and practices they have in common with peoples of other civilizations."[9]

In these words of Huntington's I see nothing less than a description of the "global ethic" project: "The future of peace and civilization depends on leading politicians and intellectuals in the major world cultures understanding each other and cooperating with each other." So Huntington ought to be able to agree: the model for the future should not be a clash and conflict of cultures, but dialogue and cooperation among cultures.

NOTES

1. Cf. H. Küng (with J. van Ess, H. v. Stietencron, H. Bechert), *Christianity and the World Religions. Paths of Dialogue with Islam, Hinduism, and Buddhism.*(New York: Doubleday, 1987; London: SCM Press, 1993), Epilogue.
2. UNESCO colloquium "World Religions, Human Rights and World Peace," Paris, 8-10 February 1989. H. Küng-K.-J. Kuschel (Eds.), Weltfrieden durch Religionsfrieden. Antworten aus den Weltreligionen (Munich: Piper Verlag, 1993)
3. H. Küng, *Global Responsibility: In Search of a New Ethic* (London: SMC Press, 1991; New York: Continuum, 1993).
4. Cf. S.P. Huntington, "The Clash of Civilizations?," *Foreign Affairs* 72, no. 3 (1993), 22-49.

   For a first critical reaction, cf. H. Küng, *Christianity. Its Essence and History.* (London: SCM Press, 1995; New York: Continuum, 1995), chapter C.V, 9: "Tasks for an analysis of postmodernity: A war of civilizations?"

5. On the argument with Henry Kissinger cf. H. Küng, *A Global Ethic for Global Politics and Economics* (London: SCM Press, 1997; New York: Oxford University Press, 1998), pp. 3-14.
6. S.P. Huntington, *The Clash of Civilizations* (New York: Simon & Schuster, 1996); German: *Der Kampf der Kulturen* (Munich: Europaverlag, 1996).
7. Ibid. p.312.
8. Ibid. p.321.
9. Ibid. p.320.

CHAPTER 10

International Morality and Cross-Cultural Bridging

Bassam Tibi

STUDENTS OF ISLAMIC CIVILIZATION and its history are familiar with the distinguishing title *al-Mu'allim al-thani* (the second master) coined for the foremost founder of political philosophy in Islam, al-Farabi (870–950).[1] Muslim contemporaries of al-Farabi ranked him second *(al-thani)* while reserving the first ranking—*al-Mu'allim al-awwal*—to a non-Muslim: Aristotle.[2] Similarly, Europeans value the Muslim philosophers Ibn Sina (Latin: Avicenna) (980–1035) and Ibn Rushd (Latin: Averroës) (1126–1198) not only for their transmitting of Greek legacy in an Islamic shape to Europe, but also for their own epistemological accomplishments, such as Ibn Rushd's teaching about the *Haqiqa al-muzdawaja* (double truth). This Ibn Rushdian insight differentiates between philosophical, that is reason-based knowledge, and religious beliefs based on divine revelation and thus paved the way for establishing modern rationalism. The inference from this introductory notion is that Islam and the West are indebted to one another.

THE POSITIVE LEGACY

The preeminent historian of civilizations, Leslie Lipson, refers to the intellectual Islamic impact on the emerging West at the eve of the Renaissance and puts the issue in this way: "Aristotle crept back into Europe by the side door. His return was due to the Arabs, who had become acquainted with Greek thinkers. . . . Both Avicenna and Averroës were influenced by him. When the University of Paris was organized, Aristotle was introduced from Cordoba."[3]

The internationally leading Islamologue Maxime Rodinson addresses the attraction of Muslim Cordoba and Toledo to the West in terms of "La fascination de l'Islam."[4] It is this very spirit of Cordoba that inspired Holocaust survivor and preeminent publisher Lord George Weidenfeld to invite major opinion leaders from Judaism, Christianity, and Islam to convene in Cordoba in February 1998 to establish a trialogue among these communities in the pursuit of peace. Having had the honor of being among the speakers in that trialogue, I argued in my presentation there that we are the contemporaries of the age of conflict between civilizations, and then inferred that we should place our discourse in this context as a means of peaceful conflict resolution. I introduce my comments on the contributions of President Herzog with these remarks, because they—as references—delineate the framework of my thoughts. In the ensuing deliberations the significance of these references will be made clear.

The German President Roman Herzog—who four years ago honored me in decorating me with the First Class Medal of the State, for mediating between Islam and the West—is deeply concerned about peace and thus reluctant to qualify our world time as an age of conflict between civilizations. His thoughts—as expressed in the collected papers of this volume—are centered around the search for commonalities for "Preventing the Clash of Civilizations." I share the concern of President Herzog as well as his search for commonalities, but maintain, however, that we should not overlook areas of conflict. In line with President Herzog I emphasize the meaning of dialogue, which I view as an instrument of conflict resolution. In the ensuing reasoning about this issue I shall ask questions, on the top of which are: Is the aspired prevention of a clash of civilizations manageable?, and, if the answer is yes, then How?

AN EFFORT TO RECONCILE THE APPROACHES OF HERZOG AND HUNTINGTON

The internationally renowned scholar of Harvard, Samuel P. Huntington, shares the German President's concern about the search for commonalities and therefore concludes his book *The Clash of Civilizations* with a chapter on "The Commonalties of Civilizations."[5] Nevertheless, the focus of Huntington is much different from the one pursued by Herzog. While Herzog is at pains to play down all kinds of dissent, Huntington—conversely—elaborates on sources of divergence leading to international conflict. Herzog underlines "sharing values" (speech of April 5, 1995) in the context of "the common heritage of Islamic and Western cultures," whereas Huntington identifies the points of difference. Who is right? Is there a middle way? Could we relate both views to one another to deal with pending issues?

Being a person of an Arab Muslim upbringing with an academic training in Germany and the United States, living in the West as a migrant in Germany and a visiting scholar at Harvard, I do experience in my daily life more differences than commonalities between Western and Islamic civilization. Are these tensions temporary and rather political? Or do they have a cultural underpinning?

I started my comments with a reference to the Islamic reverence for Aristotle and the high ranking attributed to him in the Islamic past to provide a historical example. I also wanted to present a model for common understanding in the future, without denying the reality of either existing tough anti-Westernism in contemporary Islamic civilization[6] or the spreading Islamophobia[7] in the West.

Being a Muslim migrant with German citizenship, I highly appreciate the honorable will of the German President to prevent a clash between civilizations and—moreover—share it. But, as an International Relations scholar who makes an effort to combine pragmatism and ethics I cannot overlook the existing conflict potentials in the interaction between civilizations in the post-bipolar age at the turn of the millennium. In other words: the good intention does not relieve us of the task to analyze these potentials for equipping ourselves with the means of peaceful conflict resolution. I reiterate my view that inter-cultural dialogue is a means for conflict resolution. Therefore, it is not just an intellectual exchange or even a useless "nice" conversation.

In Spring 1995 President Herzog visited one of the largest Islamic nations, Pakistan, and delivered in Islamabad his distinguished speech on the common Islamic-Western heritage while distancing himself from Huntington's concept of a clash of civilizations. In the Fall of the very same year the German Cultural Center in Karachi, Pakistan organized a big event on dialogue between Islam and the West with the subtitle "How to deal with differences."[8] Having been among the speakers, I, in three presentations delivered there, pinpointed in the debates several areas of "difference" that could lead to conflict. The issue areas are: secular nation-state versus divine order, individual human rights versus religious duties, and, in Islamic migration to Europe, integration versus communitarianism.[9] Of course, there are peaceful solutions for all of these conflict areas. My point is, however, that there are not only commonalities, but also dividing differences that need to be taken into consideration. It is not only a matter of honesty, but also of policy- and decision-making to refer to these conflictful issues to be in a position to solve them.

On the presented grounds my argument is: It is possible—and even necessary—to strive for a synthesis between the differing approaches of President Herzog and Professor Huntington. By this I mean a synthesized approach that combines an analysis of the undeniable conflict between civilizations with an ethical search for cross-cultural commonalities. The result would be a strategy of inter-cultural dialogue that goes beyond moralistic pronouncements and stands in the service of peaceful conflict resolution. In this context I am inclined to repeat the "Karachi Formula": Dialogue means "how to deal with differences." This should be set as a target in the needed effort at dialogue. In Karachi, and other comparable Western-Islamic dialogues conducted in Jakarta, Kuala Lumpur, Amman and elsewhere, the points of difference were addressed not in the sense of dividing fault lines, but in the spirit of a framework related to a strategy of searching for solutions and commonalities. In this sense I believe in the need to combine the approaches of Herzog and Huntington, not to entrench, or even divorce them from one another.

HOW TO ADDRESS THE ISSUES WITHOUT DEMONIZATION?

At this point, I must acknowledge that moralistic German intellectuals are currently demonizing every talk about "difference."[10] In this context Huntington has been greatly demonized. There are many books and articles in which *Gesinnungsethiker* try to prohibit critical reasoning. It is a fact, however, that the German edition of Huntington's book has the misleading title *Kampf der Kulturen* (Struggle between Cultures). Nevertheless, the German translation has sold more than one hundred thousand copies.

As a Muslim mediating between Islam and the West I do not share the venue of demonization and consider it dangerous and disturbing. I believe that this as well as any other kind of demonization is counter-productive for our debate. In this regard I thank President Herzog and his associates for attempting to include Huntington in this volume and very much regret that he declined the invitation. Having referred to my Islamic cultural background and Western education, I—as a person living between both civilizations—cannot overlook the very deep differences that do exist. In my work, I address these differences (see notes 10 and 20). At this juncture I am close to Huntington in stating the situation of conflict between civilizations, but of course refer to conflict only in the pursuit of peaceful dialogueic solutions. In the latter intention I am close to President Herzog. However, the very fact that I am addressing points of difference has led to extending the demonization of Huntington to my own person and work. I infer from this nuisance the need for a rational debate on pending issues that would transcend the taboos and censorship[11] of political correctness. The matter is too valuable: world peace should be kept out of polemics and moralizing pronouncements.

Conflictful matters between Islam and the West primarily revolve around two issue areas: power and values. I follow

President Herzog in focusing on the normative level of the debate and thus on values as the major subject in the inter-cultural dialogue. For this reason the remainder of the present comments deals with values, value-change, and international morality, with a focus on cross-cultural bridging. In leaning on President Herzog, I present an alternative way to look at the interrelations between culture/civilization, development, and globalization.[12] In my thoughts culture is defined as a social production of meaning, that is as a local setup.[13] Similar and related cultures group together to form civilizations in our global village. In overcoming the inherited dichotomy of tradition/modernity and the related evolutionist view on unilinear progress, the European expansion is not only conceptualized in terms of creating a Eurocentric world economy, but also and in the first place as an effort to shape the world along the lines of Western civilization and its standards. At the end of the millennium the backlash to the penetration by the modernization-acculturation-Westernization project assumes the shape of re-traditionalization, counter-acculturation, and de-Westernization. The backlash may be viewed as an expression of a clash of civilizations. Regardless of the position taken we certainly need to acknowledge Huntington's effort to bring culture/civilization into the analysis and also to appreciate this but without the West-centric bias implied in Huntington's views. Unlike Huntington I do not view the conflict in terms of security analysis, but rather as a conflict between civilizational worldviews that can be averted through the search for a cross-cultural, that is not universalist morality. I do, however, appreciate Huntington's acknowledgment of our culturally multifaceted world and also his search for commonalities. In short, my position lies between Herzog and Huntington, and I view myself as rather a mediator between them.

In fact, what leads to an actualization of a clash of civilizations—aside from its existing potential—is the politicization of civilizational worldviews that results in the political ideologies of religious fundamentalisms.[14] International morality is presented as an alternative that aims at cross-cultural bridging, not at a clash. Religious fundamentalists politicize differences and thus move the clash of civilizations from the potential to the actual. To be sure, this actual clash is still not at the level of military assaults, of course, for which fundamentalists of any kind lack the needed capabilities, but rather on the level of clashing worldviews. In contrast, the search for commonalities—without denying differences—is a contribution for preventing the clash of civilizations.

THE FOCAL ISSUE OF THE DEBATE

Islamic-Western relations are as old as the history of the Islamic presence in the Mediterranean. Recent is the new global context. For this reason we at first need to consider the altered setup in Western Islamic relations. In our age change is no longer simply an issue that concerns individual societies. The reasons for this are not only the widely discussed processes of globalization. These processes compel us to reconsider hitherto inherited concepts, to overcome their clearly limited frameworks and traditional wisdoms. Basically, in our global age issues of cultures and civilizations are moving to center stage. Just a few decades ago students were exposed to the evolutionist schemes of change, from tradition to modernity, that only allowed something in between to be grasped in terms of states of transition between traditional and modern societies.[15] Thus values were considered to be either traditional or modern or those of the passing societies. Of course, there existed challenges to these schemes—such as those presented by the critical theory of the Frankfurt School. However, the challengers were not less Eurocentric in their views than those they supposedly challenged.

The great French social scientist Raymond Aron was among the very few scholars able to honor the social fact of cultural diversity as clearly resistant to the standardization effects of a globalizing world. This globalization has been described in terms of the "shrinking of the globe" to the extent of becoming a "global village." Yet, *there is no parallel global culture* in sight. Aron addressed the issue of cultural diversity in terms of a "heterogeneity of civilizations"[16] that has been superseded and superficially veiled only by the international structures of bipolarity and the related competition among the former superpowers. In his great work *Paix et guerre entre les nations,* published in 1962, Aron was quite sure that this imposed veil of bipolarity was not a lasting one. At the turn of the century we are witnessing the return of civilizations to center stage, yet in a different shape and, of course, under radically different conditions. Huntington has been the one who brought the issue to the fore, but certainly did not invent it, as his foes contend.

Among my basic contentions is the view that cultures and civilizations are different settings. I contend that every civilization has its own sets of worldviews that determine the values of the people belonging to each of these civilizations. The fact that these worldviews and their related values differ and may conflict with one another seems quite natural. Seen from a Western point of view, we might be able to study change in the area of values with the assistance of general concepts and theories. It is, however, imperative to honor the fact that in each case cultural and civilizational sets of values are involved. If the view is accepted that knowledge is universal we may look at this point of view as a general one. Nevertheless, these values cannot be simply described as either "modern" or "traditional" or be reduced to socioeconomic constraints in a mechanistic, that is reductionist, manner. In these comments I shall argue that there exists an interplay between cultural, socioeconomic, and political change. Men and women are embedded in these intricate processes and have their own culturally determined perceptions. Cultural perceptions are not always mechanistic reflections of an objective reality inasmuch as they themselves can share existing realities and affect them. For this reason the study of values in the process of change needs to be freed from existing reductionist approaches. I propose to add these insights to the plea of sharing values proposed by President Herzog. In the pursuit of inter-civilizational dialogue the insight is pivotal that cultural values are mutable, that is, subject to change.

IS GLOBALIZATION WESTERNIZATION?

There are basic, but not *essential,* Western or Islamic values. We need to study change in values in our age. Such change is not only linked to structural globalization, but also to the fact that our century could be described as an "age of extremes," to borrow the term coined by Eric Hobsbawm. Our age is also the age of value conflicts between civilizations with differing worldviews. The European expansion has not only been an expansion of modern economic structures, in that it has also been related to the claim to Westernize the world in the course of sweeping modernization. Within this context the study of change in the non-Western parts of the world has been conceived as a study of societies moving from tradition to modernity. In this process they were supposed to adopt Western values believed to be universal and thus valid for the entire world and all of its civilizations. In this understanding, European expansion has been related to claims and processes of modernization, acculturation, and Westernization.[17] All of these three concepts were hitherto wittingly or unwittingly used interchangeably. For this reason non-Western peoples are distrustful—aside from diplomatic courtesies—when asked to join a dialogue with the West about common values. Given these obstacles, it is wise to acknowledge that dialogue is not a swift and untroubled business.

In the Western debate some basic insights have been blatantly missing. In the first place, the conceptualization of culture in terms of tradition and modernity, as well as the perception of processes of change in terms of unilinear development directed towards more progress, were based on a misconception. The claim to the universal validity of all Western assumptions has been an impediment in the way of better, that is, more accurate, knowledge about non-Western civilizations. An accurate understanding is needed. As Aron put it, *people belong to cultures and civilizations with their own worldviews and values.*

The processes of modernization inherent in the ongoing globalization cannot undo the existence of cultural and civilizational diversity. In fact, the shrinking of the world to a global village has led to an unprecedented mutual awareness and interaction among peoples of different cultures and civilizations, but it can not "in itself create a unity of outlook and has not in fact done so" as Hedley Bull rightly argued.[18] The mutual awareness on global grounds has not led to cultural standardization, but rather to the opposite: an awareness of being different. Thus, the result has been an assertive awareness of the values of one's own civilization. From these processes the values- and norms-centered "Revolt against the West"[19] grew and has moved to center stage. Long before the end of the East-West conflict Hedley Bull made in this regard a clear distinction. At issue is the differentiation of the early anticolonial revolt against the West that used Western concepts (for example, popular sovereignty and the nation-state) to legitimize the drive to national independence from the new "Revolt against the West" (see note 19). The latter—as already pointed out—is a revolt against Western values and against their claim to universality. The formula "Krieg der Zivilisationen/War of Civilizations,"[20] used as a title for my book on this subject, addresses exactly this issue as a matter of fact and not as a simple allegation.

To be sure, my approach is different from that of the Huntingtonian clash of civilizations. My concept of "war of civilizations" departs from the fact that civilizations have no armies and cannot revolve around a core-state to compete for world power, as Huntington contends. My research interest revolves around worldviews and values and thus I share with President Herzog the will to find a formula for value sharing. The tough question is how?

The contended "war of civilizations" is a war of conflicting worldviews that either claim universality for themselves or contest the claim of others to universality as imposed on them. Given that no one and discrete civilizational universalism can underpin a globally valid consensus, politicians like President Herzog who are committed to world peace are challenged to look for possible alternatives. I believe that the concept of international morality as presented in these comments may qualify for being an apt ground for an inter-civilizational consensus on basic values. To be sure, this international morality is not the "world ethos" coined by Hans Küng. In my view, there exists in reality no world ethos, because each civilization has its own ethos underpinned by a respective worldview. At this point I also question President Herzog's notion of "world civilization."

STRUCTURAL GLOBALIZATION, BUT SIMULTANEOUSLY A CULTURAL FRAGMENTATION, THUS NO UNIVERSALIZATION

At the end of the millennium, the expected processes of modernization, acculturation, and Westernization of the world seem to be reversed into processes of re-traditionalization, counter-acculturation and de-Westernization. It is intriguing to see that the revival of local cultures and the civilizations around which they revolve is related to a multifaceted simultaneity.

First, despite of its distinctive nature, the awakening of premodern cultures—believed to be "parochial"—and of the traditional civilizations such as Islam, Hinduism, Confucianism is embedded in the very same context. It is a context for which the established terms "world time" and the "global village" have been coined. However, globalization is basically different from universalization.

Second, those structures that have been unfolding in the Western civilization are globalizing. In the time span of centuries the European expansion has been the framework for globalization, but the values of the very same civilization are not universalizing simultaneously. As long as this distinction is not being understood well, the outcome of a simultaneity of structural globalization and cultural fragmentation, that is the coexistence of global structures and dissent over values, will be beyond comprehension.

A basic requirement is needed for understanding the described setup alluded to and conceptualized in terms of simultaneity of unifying structures and separating outlooks, that is decline in the consensus about common interests and values within the international system.[21] This requirement is to *honor the existing heterogeneity of civilizations.* Unlike others, in my work I make a clear distinction between culture and civilization, I do not use them interchangeably. In my terminology—as explained above—culture is conceived of as a setup for the social production of meaning with the conclusion that cultures are always local (see note 13). However, cultures can belong to a grouping, in that they may have a family resemblance in terms of values and worldviews. This family grouping is here called a civilization. In this understanding there exists only one Western and also only one Islamic civilization. In Islam, there is no one unique culture, but thousands of cultures; there exists, however, one Islamic civilization. In other words: both Western and Islamic civilization are subdivided into a great variety of local cultures. In my study of Islam I have addressed this setup in terms of a simultaneity of civilizational unity and cultural diversity. With regard to the prevailing worldview, the culturally different peoples of Islamic civilization share the very same civilizational patterns vis-à-vis the West. Nevertheless, their values, even though they may differ, are closer to one another than to the values of Western and other civilizations. In this regard my views are similar to those of Huntington. I argue that throughout the world of Islam the imposition of Western universalism in the name of modernization is being contested. Peace in the "global village" requires international consensus on values; inter-cultural dialogue, as envisaged by President Herzog, is an instrument for peaceful conflict resolution.

The ongoing globalization generates processes of change in which values are embedded. In this context I identify three levels for the needed dialogue, the local-cultural, the regional-civilizational, and the global one. A mediation between these three levels is imperative for world peace. Only in this manner may we achieve President Herzog's goal to avert a clash. Mutual awareness of difference does not necessarily have to lead to strife. It also can lead to a mutual understanding with the clear will to live in peace with one another. Cultural dialogue in the pursuit of the search for value commonality, that is for international morality, is more promising than the imposition of a universalism of one civilization on the others. However, unlike President Herzog I stress the fact that we need to address points of difference. In my inquiry I view cultural dialogue—understood in this manner—as a means for the search for common values and for establishing a value consensus in terms of international morality. This process is addressed as a shift from universalisms to an effort to create a cross-cultural underpinning that will bridge competing and rival and thus potentially clashing civilizations. My work on human rights in Islamic civilization is an example of how this cross-cultural bridging can be the alternative to a sweeping Western universalism (see note 23).

At issue is the inclination to reduce the ever-increasing cultural fragmentation in international society. At this juncture it seems useful to me to introduce a basic differentiation used in the study of international relations for understanding the structural unity and paralleling disunity or fragmentation in the realm of values. The systemic interlinking of the different parts of the world to one another in the context of the globalization of the European institution of the nation-state has resulted in the emergence of the *international system of states.* Unlike this international system of formal interaction, an *international society,* that is a society of states, "exists when a group of states, conscious of certain common interests and common values . . . conceive of themselves to be bound by a common set of rules in their relations with one another."[22] No prudent observer would deny the existence of universal rules in the international system even though the relations between the states forming this system are more or less based on formal interaction. It follows that our world is a mixture of an interactive system and a norms- and values-centered society, even though both cannot be equated with one another.

In relating the concept of *international morality* to the described realities of an international system of states and an accompanying international society, the search for common values in a changing world is to be grasped as an effort to bridge the space between the system and society, to bring them closer to one another. The imperative of honoring the natural and historically developed subdivision of humanity into local cultures and regional civilizations and of relating this needed insight to the realities of international relations leads to viewing groups of states as civilizational state communities. In so doing, I do not follow Samuel Huntington, who replaces the earlier existing state blocs of the bipolar world with the envisaged new state blocs of civilizations. It is extremely difficult to identify one or more core states in each civilization as a leading power. In Islamic civilization this is quite impossible. Civilizations are too diverse in their inner relations and thus may not allow such a structure as that envisaged by Huntington. However, in their external relations, civilizations emphasize their common values. The resulting value conflicts may be addressed for instance as a conflict between Western-Asian or Western-Islamic values. The alternative to basing these value conflicts as new grounds for international relations, as Huntington does, is my proposition to establish an inter-cultural and inter-civilizational dialogue as a means for the search for common values, that is international morality on cross-cultural, mutual, not imposed, universalistic grounds. In the pursuit of democracy and human rights this cross-cultural approach seems to be more promising than any universalism.

FUTURE PROSPECTS

The approach of President Herzog to establish a dialogue between civilizations needs to be placed in the context of several well known international projects in which scholars from different civilizations have committed themselves to the perspective that the existing "heterogeneity of civilizations" should not lead to a clash between them. For averting the potential of such a clash the idea of a core of values has risen and been promoted as a binding commitment. At the center of these values believed to become possibly common are secular democracy and individual human rights. One of the contributions of President Herzog collected in this volume is a remarkable essay on human rights (chapter 3).

On the examples of earlier pursued international projects I want to allude to the issue of how to establish the cross-cultural human rights approach. At the Wilson Center in Washington, D.C., and at the Norwegian Institute for Human Rights the idea for establishing a cross-cultural, instead of a universalistic, underpinning of these values created the ground on which I have developed my concept of international morality.[23] In a further effort to pursue this line of reasoning I have participated in the project of Democracy and Democratization in Asia conducted at the Université Catholique de Louvain/Belgium.[24] In all three projects international scholars agreed on cross-cultural grounds on the possibility of bridging the civilizations; they conceded that an ethical potential is available for an agreement on common values. The views of President Herzog are congenial and very close to those of the involved scholars.

The assumption of cross-cultural bridging acknowledges the differences existing between local cultures and between regional civilizations. Political correctness and cultural nihilism, in contrast, deny these realities. In fact, these political correctness–driven attitudes of blinding oneself vis-à-vis cultural differences are a highly risky and self-defeating way of dealing with realities in which cultures and civilizations are moving center stage. I have already referred to the very important Islamic-Western dialogue run in Karachi, where the basic formula for this dialogue was "how to deal with differences." The very same can be said about the Jakarta dialogue also mentioned above.[25] In order to further pursue this goal, one needs first to be in a position to acknowledge these differences. To find ways for dealing with them is the substance of the dialogue—an instrument to avert a clash of civilizations. It thus follows, that an effort to deny differences will subsequently undermine a fruitful dialogue.

In the course of my involvement in a variety of international projects concerned with these issues I have learned that there are basically two ways to deal with differences. The first is to politicize the different worldviews and the values that emerge from the heterogeneity of civilizations. This results in the political ideology of religious fundamentalisms now unfortunately spreading throughout the world (see note 14) and is the scenario described as the "war of civilizations" (see note 20). To be sure and to reiterate: it is not a war conducted with military means, but rather on the ground of rival worldviews. The second approach is to recognize that differences can be addressed within the framework of an inter-cultural bridging.

In summing up, the great challenge at the turn of the century is a challenge to rethink old wisdoms and to develop new insights. I share President Herzog's search for "sharing values," I highlight however the argument that the earlier approaches to the study of values in terms of tradition and modernity within the framework of an evolutionist belief in progress can no longer provide convincing answers for the pending tough questions. Values are related to cultures and civilizations and they differ from one another. Thus sharing values needs cross-cultural underpinning.

Change in our age is a change toward more globalization. However, globalization is a more intrinsic and complicated issue than the American belief in a standardized McWorld-culture suggests. McWorld in the sense that our world is "McDonaldizing," that is culturally standardizing, is clearly a misperception. It is silly to view the revolt against the West as a "Jihad versus McWorld."[26] There is a need to accept the reality Aron called in 1962 the "heterogeneity of civilizations." It follows that the existing heterogeneity of civilizations is a heterogeneity of values and the related worldviews. It is up to the involved peoples, especially scholars and policy-makers, whether or not the real dissent over values will result in a "clash of civilizations" or in the emergence of international morality.

A basic insight presented in this paper for making the needed choice is the recognition of the fact that the change in structures, globalization, is leading to an adverse state of affairs, that is fragmentation in values as related to the evolving civilization-awareness among different peoples. Inter-cultural and inter-civilizational dialogue over values—as envisaged by President Herzog—seems to be the more promising avenue for meeting the challenge than the political correctness–driven silencing of talk about differences in a time when fundamentalists are turning these differences into trenches. It is to be hoped that this volume will promote the international debate on the pending issues and thus contribute to world peace. President Herzog is to be congratulated for his efforts toward this end. President Herzog is among the unfortunately few, but very laudable, Western politicians familiar with the positive encounters between the West and Islam alluded to at the outset of these comments. President Herzog's reference to the "common heritage" of both civilizations is a good start for a dialogue that should recognize that addressing points of difference and dissent will only help to avert a clash of civilizations.

NOTES

1. See the seminal work of al-Farabi in the Arabic original *(al-Madina al-fadila)* with an English translation by Richard Walzer, *al-Farabi on the Perfect State* (Oxford: Clarendon Press, 1985). On al-Farabi see also Bassam Tibi, *Der wahre Imam: Der Islam von Mohammed bis zur Gegenwart* (Munich: Piper Press, 1996), chapter 4.
2. For the place of Aristotle in Islamic political philosophy see *The Political Aspects of Islamic Philosophy: Essays in Honor of Muhsin S. Mahdi,* edited by Charles E. Butterworth (Cambridge, MA: Harvard University Press, 1992).
3. Leslie Lipson, *The Ethical Crises of Civilization* (Newbury Park, CA: Sage, 1993), 62.
4. Maxime Rodinson, *La fascination de l'Islam* (Paris: Maspero, 1987).
5. Samuel P. Huntington, *The Clash of Civilizations and the Remaking of World Order* (New York: Simon and Schuster, 1996), final chapter.
6. Ali M. Jarisha and Muhammad Sh. Zaibaq, *Asalib al-ghazu al-fikri li'l alam al-Islami* (Methods of Intellectual Invasion of the Islamic World) (Cairo: Dar al-I'tisam, 1978).
7. Norman Daniel, *Islam and the West: The Making of an Image* (Oxford: One World, 1993).
8. See the report by S. Ahmed, "Ways to Avert Clash between Islam and the West Stressed," in *DAWN* (Karachi), October 27, 1995, and in the same paper, "Cross-Cultural Talks for Peaceful Coexistence Urged," October 26, 1995.
9. See B. Tibi's chapter in the collected papers of the Karachi dialogue published under the title *Is There a Clash of Cultures?* (Karachi: 1998), 9-23; and also the interview with B. Tibi by Themina Ahmed, "The Clash of Civilizations

Was Not Invented, but It Was Used, Abused for other Reasons," in *NEWSLINE* (Karachi), November, 1995, 99-100.

10. Bassam Tibi, *Europa ohne Identitaet? Die Krise der multikulturellen Gesellschaft* (Munich: Bertelsmann, 1998), chapters 9 and 10.
11. On the German taboos see Arnulf Baring, *Scheitert Deutschland?* (Stuttgart: DVA Press, 1997), 289ff.
12. On globalization see Barrie Axford, *The Global System* (New York: St. Martin's Press, 1995).
13. See Clifford Geertz, *The Interpretation of Cultures* (New York: Basic Books, 1973) and B. Tibi, *Islam and the Cultural Accommodation of Social Change* (Boulder, CO: Westview, 1990).
14. Bassam Tibi, *The Challenge of Fundamentalism: Political Islam and the New World Disorder* (Berkeley/Los Angeles: University of California Press, 1998).
15. See the classic by David Apter, *The Politics of Modernization* (Chicago: Chicago University Press, 1965).
16. Raymond Aron, *Paix et guerre entre les nations* (Paris: 1962; German translation, Frankfurt/Main: Fischer Press, 1986).
17. Theodore H. von Laue, *World Revolution of Westernization* (New York: 1987).
18. Hedley Bull, *The Anarchical Society: A Study of Order in World Politics* (New York: Columbia University Press, 1977), 273.
19. H. Bull, "The Revolt against the West," in *The Expansion of International Society,* edited by Hedley Bull and Adam Watson (Oxford: Oxford University Press, 1984), 217-228.
20. B. Tibi, *Krieg der Zivilisationen* (Hamburg: HoCa Press, 1995; expanded and revised second edition Munich: Heyne, 1998).
21. B. Tibi, *The Challenge of Fundamentalism,* chapter 5.
22. H. Bull, *The Anarchical Society,* 13.
23. See B. Tibi, "Islamic Law/Shari'a, Human Rights, Universal Morality and International Relations," *Human Rights Quarterly* (John Hopkins University Press) 16, no. 2 (1994), 277-299; and earlier by the same author, "The European Tradition of Human Rights and the Culture of Islam," in *Human Rights in Africa,* edited by Abdullahi A. An-Na'im and Francis M. Deng (Washington, D.C.: Brookings, 1990), 104-132. See also B. Tibi, "Islamic Shari'a and Human Rights—International Law and International Relations," in *Islamic Law Reform and Human Rights,* edited by Tore Lindholm and Kari Vogt (Oslo and Copenhagen: 1993), 75-96.
24. See Michéle Schmiegelow, ed., *Democracy in Asia* (New York: St. Martin's Press, 1997), in particular the chapter by B. Tibi, "Democracy and Democratization in Islam," 127-146.
25. See notes 8 and 9 above as well as the contributions in Bahasa Indonesia by B. Tibi, S. P. Huntington, and many Indonesian authors in Nasir Tamara, ed., *Agama dan Dialogue Antar Peradaban* (Jakarta: 1996).
26. Benjamin Barber, *Jihad vs. McWorld* (New York: Ballantine, 1996).

CHAPTER 11

The Clash of Moral Value Systems

A Genuine Crisis to Be Avoided at All Costs

Masakazu Yamazaki

TODAY, WITH COLD-WAR CONFRONTATION behind us, we are witnessing the emergence of a new set of competing principles, namely, the principle of globalizing financial markets and the principle of the nation state, which presupposes the existence of borders. The battle spreads out covering arguments about the increase and distribution of wealth; the ethics of competition versus the ethics of equality; the rival demands for freedom and stability; the simultaneity of the present versus historical time; and universal rationality against cultural diversity.

When communism was still a threat, capitalism encouraged the amassing of greater wealth through free competition while also seeking to equalize affluence through redistribution. The main proponents of capitalism at the time were states, which guaranteed fair-market competition and lessened the disparity between winners and losers through taxes and welfare policies.

States sometimes became competing entities on world markets themselves, introducing regulations to constrain international competition and protect domestic industries. The role of the nation state since its inception has been to protect its own citizens and prevent excessive rivalry among them, but what particularly strengthened this role was clearly the pressure of communism.

Communism sought to disrupt states through the concept of class, replacing national borders with the ideology of international worker solidarity. Opposing this was capitalism, which needed the ideology of the state more than ever to avoid class division and to hold fast to its workers. The preeminent issue was whether people belonged to a class or to the state, and capitalism did all it could to induce people to identify themselves as members of the latter. The industrial nations of the twentieth century discarded the universalist ideals of imperialism, supported the independence of new states, and advanced the cause of democracy, which encouraged public participation in the political process. They sought to unite the people psychologically through education and cultural policies, using antitrust legislation and progressive taxes to restrain those who sought to rise above others, and through welfare policies to prevent anyone from falling too far below others.

The archetypical—and also perhaps extreme—example of these efforts can be seen in post–World War II Japan. Defeated, Japan lost the power it once had to unite its people, and domestic public opinion became neatly divided along Cold War lines on such issues as foreign policy, security, and public safety; the bulk of the news media and about a third of the National Diet supported the East camp. The Japan Socialist Party, the largest opposition party, did not recognize the legitimacy of the Self-

Defense Forces, completely rejected the Japan-U.S. Security Treaty, and refused to acknowledge the existence of the regime in Seoul, which was recognized by the Japanese government. The Japanese Communist Party, meanwhile, which called for a fundamental overthrow of the state apparatus, was allowed to operate legally, and labor unions waged a series of political struggles. Where post-war Germany was divided by a stone wall, Japan was split by a wall made of paper (newspapers, political leaflets, and so on).

The policies adopted by the government relentlessly sought to achieve economic equality and avoid turmoil. Various efforts were made to expand the economic pie and ensure "fair" distribution, such as protecting and fostering companies through industrial policy, maintaining highly progressive taxes and high inheritance tax rates, assisting farmers by keeping rice prices high and offering subsidies, and stabilizing employment through public works projects. Because corporate bankruptcies, and particularly the collapse of financial institutions, were thought to trigger social unrest, administrative guidance was strengthened to avoid these crises. Companies also sought a family type of conciliation between management and labor by adopting lifetime employment and a seniority-based wage system, and by developing business practices that gave priority to the voice of the workers over investors in management decision-making.

This produced a strange society with an extremely large government that displayed little political leadership. The government looked after its citizens like a parent but did not exercise parental authority. Politicians were respected for their ability to reconcile and compromise as opposed to displaying bold, visionary leadership. In order to avoid confrontation, making decisions became a time-consuming process, and the country began shying away from playing a salient role in international politics. Regulations to curb economic competition increased, but the government endeavored to cloak its authority. Power and responsibility became dispersed, and a faceless bureaucratic structure began to spread.

Even after communism collapsed, Japan's system, designed specifically to ward off communism, failed to adapt to this change. For Germany, where a stone wall was torn down, the challenge was to unify and bring equality to the peoples of Eastern and Western Germany, but in Japan the tearing down of the paper wall produced a challenge to mitigate the strong unity of the people and encouraged diversification. While neither task is easy, weakening the unity of the people through state leadership is almost a contradiction in terms. The systemic reforms made so far, such as the opening of Japanese markets to international competition, relaxing regulations, and simplifying the administrative structure has taken much time, but reforming the national ethic is likely to be more difficult. Japan faces a long struggle ahead to shift the focus of values away from equality and toward competition, to strengthen the principles of personal decision-making and self-accountability, to value individual creativity over conciliation with others, and to restore respect for leadership and the spirit of noblesse oblige.

However, a more fundamental problem for the post–Cold War world is exactly the opposite of the difficulties confronting Japan. For perhaps the first time since the emergence of the nation state, capitalism, not communism is beginning to conflict with the state. Corporate conglomerates are becoming global entities, with production bases dispersed in many countries. If a nation raises its taxes or tightens its regulations, the company simply will move its factories elsewhere, and it may even change the nationality of the parent firm. Companies will flee the countries where the indirect impact of government policies causes public order to deteriorate or wages to skyrocket. Today's companies need state protection, but they now have enough power to force governments to provide this protection. The choices companies make about which country to set up in can greatly influence the policies of that country.

In the case of international finance, moreover, it has even become possible for companies to stand in direct opposition to states. A widely known instance is the battle fought and won by a massive hedge fund against the Bank of England, forcing down the pound and capturing a profit. Subsequently, short-term capital swooped down on Asian economies, triggering the biggest recession following the collapse of speculative bubbles and toppling governments. Even the United States has seen the misadventures of a hedge fund that damaged major banks, put the national economy at risk, and shook the government.

By attacking state failures in economic management, forcing governments to improve their policics and sometimes even knocking these governments down, international finance resembles the communism of old. However, it is much more formidable in that, unlike communism, the faces of the real movers are invisible, not riding in tanks but operating through computers.

While faced with this new enemy, the nation state has been stricken with a disease as old as history, namely the wealth gap between the rich and poor, which communism promised but failed to resolve, and in fact only aggravated. This gap is setting citizen against citizen, while among states and races it is spurring wars and regional conflicts. In the place of communism, ethnicism and religious fundamentalism are fanning the flames of discord over material inequities and are portraying its struggle as a spiritual cause. The forces engaged in the so-called clash of civilizations, including the Islamic and Hindu religions, Slavism, and Ireland's Protestants and Catholics, are in fact people resisting poverty.

Differences in religion and customs are not a cause of clashes unless linked with this disparity between the rich and poor. In many East Asian nations, Confucianism, Buddhism, Islam, and Christianity coexist peacefully. Conversely, an example of the conflict between the rich and poor taking on the appearance of a clash of civilizations emerged in the Black Muslim movement in the United States. The ethnic riots in Indonesia in 1998 were also the result of international finance throwing the economy into turmoil, aggravating the disparity between poor Muslims and wealthy Chinese. Fascists, who instigate violence, always exploit resentment over poverty, using beautiful words to set this aflame. The concept of clashing civilizations provides such people with an argument that can become a self-fulfilling prophecy.

Market principles function to increase the world's wealth, simultaneously providing feedback and correcting the mistaken economic policies of a nation. Japan, South Korea, and Thailand are now beginning to learn a lot from the market. However, it must not be forgotten that the market does not have the power to narrow the gap between the rich and poor and could widen it. Moreover, the market has the disadvantage of being able to operate only within the time frame of the present, giving no consideration to history or the future. It does not respect cultural traditions that quietly link people and give them a stable sense of belonging. Furthermore, because of the need to cope with the price war to promote mass-consumption and production, it tends to squander future resources and damage the environment. The only entities that will be able to redress these market defects in the foreseeable future are nation states and alliances of states, such as the European Union, as well as state-supported or -protected private nonprofit groups.

States have two aspects, being rational organizations based on laws and systems on the one hand, and behaving as a culture-based community on the other. Completely open to rational markets, a state simultaneously remains closed due to customs and a shared identity among its citizens. States have visible leaders, and people can participate in management of states. Income can be redistributed peacefully due to this shared identity and the public's sense of participation, a process that can be carried out more efficiently thanks to the state's rational systems. Given that there is a limit to human wealth and that it cannot be amassed in an instant, the current method of redistribution through assistance among states would seem the most realistic approach to achieving global equality. Moreover, the continuity and identity of the state should aid people's ability to think about their history, fostering a more ethical awareness of the cultural traditions of the human race as a whole and of the happiness of future generations.

As argued in Jane Jacobs' *Systems of Survival: A Dialogue on the Moral Foundations of Commerce and Politics*, human beings have two moral systems, a commercial ethic and a political ethic. Where they intrude on each other's territory, with politics influenced by the commercial ethic or commerce by the political ethic, various forms of confusion and injustice arise. Applying this to the current situation, the former could be called a market ethic, and the latter a state ethic. In the past, Japan undeniably adhered too strongly to a state ethic, which resulted in its failure to respond to world market trends. However, if the current market ethic became the sole standard for the human race, with states operating in line with this, the suffering of human beings would become even greater.

The illusory universalism of communism has vanished, and the human race is now facing the challenge of the practical universalism of a rational market. To deal with this, we need to preserve not civilizations (not even Western civilization with all its glories)—which are another form of universalism—but rather institutions effective in guaranteeing the pluralism of human lifestyles, which at this stage in history are nation states and the alliances among them.

About the Contributors

Roman Herzog was elected President of the Federal Republic of Germany in 1994, after a distinguished career as a legal scholar, politician, and President of the Constitutional Court of the Federal Republic of Germany. His academic interests extend beyond constitutional law to the history of ancient states and cultures. He is author of *Staaten der Frühzeit* (1988), a study of the origins and governmental forms of ancient states.

Amitai Etzioni is Professor at George Washington University. His most recent books are *The New Golden Rule* and *The Limits of Privacy.* He has served as President of the American Sociological Association and Senior Advisor to the White House. He is founder of the Communitarian Network.

Hans Küng is President of the "Weltethos" Foundation in Tübingen/Zürich. He is Professor Emeritus of Theology at the University of Tübingen and has lectured in many parts of the world as a visiting professor. Among many other works, he has written *Christianity and the World Religions* (1986/93), *Global Responsibility* (1991) and *A Global Ethic for Global Politics and Economics* (1998).

Henrik Schmiegelow is Head of the Foreign Policy Department of the Office of the President of the Federal Republic of Germany. His publications deal with the relation between theory and practice in politics and economics. He is the author (with

Michèle Schmiegelow) of *Strategic Pragmatism: Japanese Lessons in the Use of Economic Theory* (1989).

Bassam Tibi is Professor of International Relations and Director of the Institute for International Relations at the Political Science Department, University of Göttingen, Germany. He currently teaches at Harvard University as Bosch Visiting Professor. His numerous books include *Conflict and War in the Middle East* (1995) and *The Challenge of Fundamentalism, Political Islam and the New World Order* (1998)

Masakazu Yamazaki is Professor at East Asia University, Shimonoseki; Director of Suntory Foundation; a playwright; and a literary critic. His many works include the sociological study *Individualism and the Japanese.* Among his most recent English publications is the article "Asia, a Civilization in the Making," which appeared in *Foreign Affairs* in 1996.